Empire and Espionage

The Anglo-Zulu War 1879

Empire and Espionage

The Anglo-Zulu War 1879

By
Stephen Wade

Pen & Sword
MILITARY

First published in Great Britain in 2010 by
Pen & Sword Military
An imprint of
Pen & Sword Books Ltd
47 Church Street
Barnsley
South Yorkshire
S70 2AS

ISBN 978 1 84884 180 2

A CIP catalogue record for this book is available from the British Library

Typeset by Acredula

Printed and bound in England
By the MPG Books Group

Pen & Sword Books Ltd incorporates the Imprints of Pen & Sword Aviation, Pen & Sword Family History, Pen & Sword Maritime, Pen & Sword Military, Wharncliffe Local History, Pen & Sword Select, Pen & Sword Military Classics, Leo Cooper, Remember When, Seaforth Publishing and Frontline Publishing

For a complete list of Pen & Sword titles please contact
PEN & SWORD BOOKS LIMITED
47 Church Street, Barnsley, South Yorkshire, S70 2AS, England
E-mail: enquiries@pen-and-sword.co.uk
Website: www.pen-and-sword.co.uk

Contents

Illustrations

Introduction

My range of reference here covers every conceivable arm of intelligence gathering in the war and beyond and ventures into the corridors of power of the politicians and diplomats. My own thinking on this diversity embraces these four definitions:

Localized Intelligence

This is any knowledge of the enemy that applies to the circumscribed area of military interest. This will of course involve border states, industry, missionary stations and police forces in the case of the Anglo-Zulu War.

Fluid Intelligence

This refers to the most common type of knowledge – that which comes and goes in the planning stage of a campaign as well as in the work done by the officers who have been allotted specific intelligence duties. I use the term to differentiate the close-contact work of scouting and reconnaissance.

Field Intelligence

This accepted term involves reconnaissance of all kinds, and also includes communication systems: hence the use of the heliograph in this war, and of course the invaluable scouting of colonial units and native contingents.

Human Intelligence ('Humint')

Nowadays, this term implies an almost antediluvian notion: that people are really at the centre of the most important information-gathering. In fact, the word, though awkward, conveys that element of person-to-person work associated with the spies in the 'Great Game' with Russia in the Indian frontier states. It applies well to Natal and Zululand in 1879 because the most effective espionage for the Zulu army was definitely humint.

These terms are simply for convenience, as military intelligence in the British colonial wars was always pragmatic, ever changing and dependent on individual initiative.

It was in the process of writing and researching for my previous book, *Spies in the Empire*, that I came to realize just how scattered, disorganized and pragmatic were the facilities in place within the Victorian imperial military regime and establishment. In that work, I was concentrating mostly on the Russian/north-west frontier context and the related buffer states. I came to see just how complex the interactions were between the political officers in the field and the diplomatic objectives at home in Whitehall. Between Wellington's wars and the first stirrings of trouble in the Kaffir War immediately before 1879, I came to see how inadequate and amateurish the intelligence methods were, highlighted most powerfully in the debacle that was the Crimean War of 1853–1856.

Much of the acceleration of intelligence measures after the Zulu conflict was still concentrated in the east, largely due to Lord Curzon, who was totally preoccupied with the threat of Russia on the Indian frontier and beyond from 1887 to the mid 1890s. I saw that, again, South Africa was bypassed in this context. This book is the result of those reflections. It became clear to me that Natal and Zululand had just as many individual and heroic figures in the military prowess exhibited in the killing grounds of Cetshwayo's kingdom. However, what I did not realize until research began was just how much the army was victim of the diplomats. Bartle Frere had already made his mark as a militant imperialist of the worst kind in other parts of the globe, and now here he was again, looking for more land and playing his own version of a kind of Empire war game with little regard for indigenous people.

With these considerations in mind, I set out to see how the war in Zululand compared with the constant skirmishes and battles in

Afghanistan and other border states in the east. I was initially appalled at the lack of preparatory theory and use of local knowledge. One of the most obvious contrasts between South Africa and India in this respect was the lack of a store of printed local information from colonists already gathered and monitored by the army. There was no such thing: merely an assemblage of magistrates, missionaries and settlers who could be called upon ad hoc. This increased the intrigue and fascination, and the result was rather a patchwork collection of stories, but hopefully this will add a little interest to the immense body of writing on the Anglo-Zulu War in print.

In many ways, the events of 1879 in South Africa were a major determining factor in shaking up attitudes at the War Office to military intelligence, both in the field and in the office back in London. As the army reforms of 1870 and 1871 had made some attempt at reconfiguring the mindset of the military within the Empire, it stressed organization and career structures (with an eye to future European threat, of course). But as for the intelligence arm of the great war machine, that was still marginal. Thanks largely to Garnet Wolseley in the Ashanti War of 1873–1874 there was some attention paid to brain rather than brawn, and more importantly it was seen that there was a need for military intelligence to have a defined place and status.

Wolseley had shown, mainly in the Ashanti War, that hand picking not only the right officers for the specific conflict was wise, but that a new breed of officer was required if wars were going to continue in which Britain fought armies in their own fields and mountains and against specialist, often unique, concepts of battle. The 'Wolseley Set' of officers were intellectuals, a new assemblage of bright young men who saw the training at the Staff College to be something fresh, an education with a broader reach than previously. This was partly because of the Franco-Prussian War of 1870–1871 in which the victorious Prussians (our allies at Waterloo, of course) had shown the value of planning and of a new rationale about what an army actually was and what it could be with the right attitudes from theoretical thinking. Wolseley's men wrote books and reports; they sketched and they absorbed local and regional knowledge. They discussed other cultures and learned Arabic or any other native tongue that would be useful. The invasion over the Tugela river came before all this had properly settled, while the Duke of Cambridge, in charge of the British Army, still felt antagonistic to Wolseley's image and ideas.

Yet when the troubles in South Africa emerged, first with the Kaffir War and then with the rise to power of Bartle Frere and the Forward Policy with an eye on Zululand, the attention was on India, not Africa. The Great Game, beginning in earnest around 1830, had accelerated by the 1870s and both the Balkan crisis of 1877 and the Second and Third Afghan Wars of 1878–1879 reinforced the view that if there were to be a testing ground for the new Intelligence Branch it should be in the Punjab and the buffer states between India and Russia, not in Africa at all.

The conflict with the mighty army of Cetshwayo changed all that. The notion of 'intelligence' had always been something commanding officers had seen as being totally ad hoc: because each theatre of war was unique, it was argued, there had to be individuated thinking on all matters of strategy when actually in the field. But after groundbreaking work by a number of officers in the 1850s, learning from the errors of the Crimea, some influential minds in military affairs began to rethink. It took remarkable individuals to effect change, notably William Robertson, Wolseley and John Maurice, Reginald Wingate and Henry Brackenbury.

The forces resistant to change in this respect were many and varied. Heroism, *esprit de corps* and all the related ideological concepts might have a place in this conservatism. Also, there was the gentlemanly objection to the word 'spy' as being something beyond the moral reach of an army man, something very foreign, European and not quite right. A cad might indulge in spying, but not an officer. However, when maverick officers such as Richard Burton and Alexander Burnes gathered a dashing notoriety, there was a slight chink of light in the curtain around the taboo notion of espionage.

On the domestic front, the first decades of Victoria's reign had brought so much radical trouble in the streets and so much violent crime as the cities grew that the new professional police were seen as

'European' – a fear based on the French police system, which had always used espionage and *agents provocateurs* to search out dissidents. But when Cardwell's reforms had shaken up the army, the more enlightened 'new men' in the officer class began to move for change in areas of the high command and in the classroom at the Staff College.

However, all this was to come too late for the Zulu War. But why have we such a massive iconic literature and filmography of this war? Arguably, it is because under the seeming chaos and the disastrous errors in leadership there was a game of soldiers, that is in the sense of a large force of disparate professionals and native levies deployed across a circumscribed area, as if the 'Game of War' that was being played back home in the mess (something invented by the Prussians) was actually being applied in the field. But of course, the 'game' in the theatre of war was a bloodbath and there were serious consequences. There has long been a comparative scholarship on war, relating the entire vocabulary of warfare to play, in particular John Huizinga's seminal work *Homo Ludens*, in which he formed the view that 'culture itself bears the character of play'. Certainly, in military leadership, because field strategy had been the province of whimsical aristocrats as well as true soldiers for many centuries, it is not difficult to see Huizinga's ideas in military actions and theories. There is something boyish about the mediation of the Zulu War battles – of course not in themselves as they really were, but in the sense of playing war games with tin soldiers. This is most obvious from the uniforms still worn by the troops in 1879 – parade-ground wear, not battle dress for that climate and terrain.

For all these reasons, the intelligence template of learning by errors may plainly be seen in Isandlwana, and that was observed at the time, of course. But what was not appreciated for some time was just how much thinking Chelmsford did. His materials in the archive, and the chronological sequence of letters and notes gathered in John Laband's book *Lord Chelmsford's Zululand Campaign 1878–1879* show just how much he tried to think ahead and prepare for every eventuality. Naturally, the basic weakness was the central tenet of all military intelligence: know the enemy.

The media coverage was eventually immense, coming after the initial stages were well advanced. After Isandlwana it seemed that everyone was an expert on Zulu affairs. The press was besieged by letters from people with all kinds of experience and expertise. So many travellers, civil servants and amateur explorers had been to various parts of Africa that they considered themselves experts and they expressed their views. This is important for understanding the nature of theoretical intelligence. Field intelligence was a different matter, but the theory of warfare and how knowledge of the enemy played a part in this had become by circa 1870 encyclopaedic in approach: that is, amass information, compile gazetteers and gather gentlemen-scholars and linguists and all will be well. The influence of Auguste Comte and Positivism cannot be overlooked in this context: the Victorians had become the heirs of Dickens' Mr Gradgrind with his teaching of precise and robotic knowledge. But having said that, it cannot be doubted that the fruits of this were extremely valuable in India and in the Great Game with Russia. After all, travellers and linguists had always been in the officer class, but this had not been channelled thoughtfully. William Robertson, one of the first men in the new Intelligence Branch of 1873, was to experience his first acquirement of intelligence skills and knowledge in the Punjab.

The Indian army, and indeed the army of the East India Company, had been the focus of the intelligence arm of the British army. Africa had been left to the amateurs such as the border agents. But the new breed of political officers, such as William Shepstone, were to establish the beginnings of more streamlined field intelligence in Africa, though admittedly it was thought at the time that the intelligence officers had been a major cause of the failure against the Boers in the wars of 1899–1902. This was not true, and the intelligence high command, headed by Sir John Ardagh, were the whipping-boys at the time. Colonel Henderson, also in a high rank against the Boers, had been a top-notch tutor at the Staff College and had taught several of the young men who were to make their mark in military intelligence.

Yet all this came too late for the war against the Zulu. The reasons for the failure of Lord Chelmsford in the confrontation leading to

Isandlwana are not hard to find. They have been well explored. It was a case of an invading army that fragmented and which had errors in field intelligence and in communications that left a large body of men vulnerable to an army that had operated as it always did: using mobility and stealth, together with the unique features of the terrain, to locate and exploit weaknesses in the enemy. This story has been told well, mainly by Ian Knight, Adrian Greaves and Saul David. Their writings have explained with great power and impact the shortcomings of the Chelmsford expedition force.

This book sets out to say little that may be added to that body of writing. It is rather a cluster of perspectives on the Zulu War, looking at several aspects of intelligence in the context of the time and the ideologies that prevailed. I also include the mediation and assessment of the Zulu War, which was even written about by the worst poet of the nineteenth century, William McGonagall, who said, writing about 'The Hero of Rorke's Drift':

> 'News from the front!' said one, 'Awful news!' said the other,
> 'Of which, we are afraid, will put us to great bother,
> For the black Zulus are coming, and for our blood doth thirst:'
> 'And the force is cut up to pieces!' shouted the first ...

The very fact that the bad poet wrote about Isandlwana, along with other momentous events of the age, tells us just how much the defeat cut into the public awareness of war – and this in an age in which wars were constant, as the massive and expanding Empire swallowed up wave after wave of administrators, troops and supporting families and servants. But the Zulu War stood out, equated with the retreat from Kabul in 1842 and the Mutiny of 1857, as a dark hour in Her Majesty's dominions. The myth ate into the truth, and I intend to explore the responses and appraisals of intelligence minds during and after the war.

I have not offered yet another set of interpretations of well-established events and neither have I narrated the sequences of actions and responses in important battles: all that has been done with great skill and knowledge by Ian Knight, Adrian Greaves and John Laband, and everyone writing on this war has to acknowledge the solid work of Donald R Morris. My objective here has been to gather every important aspect of intelligence, even down to related areas of communication and diplomacy, though naturally, in passing, I have had to summaries some events. If these short introductions to the range of field and theoretical intelligence factors in this important conflict open up debate and interest, then the purpose has been served.

1

Two Adventurers

Learning about a particular war may be done through conventional narrative: by accounts of strategy and movement or deployment of men and resources. It can be done by keeping to the big picture. But aspects of a conflict may also be highlighted if we look at the sideshows as well as at the main feature. Therefore, before looking at the official statements about the Zulu War from the Intelligence Branch, we begin with two stories.

Sackville Lane-Fox (1861–1879)

Sackville's father, Sackville Senior, was a yeomanry officer, the 12th Baron Conyers. He had three children with Mary Curteis, and Sackville, known as Sack or Jacko in the family, was born in London in 1861. In the autumn of 1878 he set off for Natal with nothing planned regarding his soldiering there. He simply knew that he wanted to join a regiment and fight the Zulu. In a letter home in December that year he wrote: 'I am going on to Natal by the American tomorrow but don't know what I am to do there. Some people say I may get a commission in a levy and some say I may be attached as a volunteer with a British regiment. If I don't get something at once I shall join one of those irregular regiments.'[1]

This points to one important aspect of the war immediately – a fact that Henry Curling commented on when he wrote, 'such numbers of officers are coming out here in search of fighting that they cannot think there is to be anything of the kind in Europe. We have got six officers in my battery now, 2 of them senior to me and there are several other gunners waiting employment …'[2] Sack was out for adventure and he was one of the many, as Curling saw. But the son of Lord Conyers had an introduction to Sir Bartle Frere, and just a short time before the Chelmsford columns advanced, he met Frere: 'Sir Bartle was very kind and asked me to dinner and offered me a room in the same house as his staff, and said he would do all he could for me – He introduced me to Major Mitchell.'[4]

Sack joined the Natal Native Infantry and he noted that he was to cross the Tugela. His words when writing home are enlightening with regard to the attitudes at the time:

> There will be a howling fight as the Zulus always come out in great masses and charge and of course they will be shot down by the thousand, but after the first fight the fun will be over and the nasty work of hunting them in the bush will begin, as they will get such a lesson that they will not show their faces in the open … The soldiers here think they will shoot a thousand of them by Sunday.[4]

The irony is huge, of course, but arguably these attitudes betray what he had heard: that is to say that other men had told a newcomer about the way the Zulu fight. These wrong-headed attitudes were part of the Chelmsford mindset and were also the talk in the tents and mess rooms. Chelmsford had written to Theophilus Shepstone in July 1878 of the Zulu: 'They must be thoroughly crushed to make them believe in our superiority, and if I am called upon to conduct operations against them, I shall strive to be in a position to show them how hopelessly inferior they are to us in fighting power …'[5]

But Sack Lane-Fox never moved further north than a dot on the map south of the Tugela. After Isandlwana, on 10 February 1879, he wrote home: 'I suppose you hear what an infernal mess we have got into. We have all bolted behind earthworks and until troops come out from England we shall never show our faces more than a mile or so from our trenches.'[6] They had dug in and cowered close to the river, and had not advanced because they could not gather a full complement of men. The other battalions had their full 1,100 men but Sack's was short, with only officers and NCOs (non-commissioned officers) and three incomplete companies.

The intelligence was by then spreading with a mix of fact and rumour. Sack was told (we do not know by who) that there was a body of Zulu numbering 1,500 strong in the rear of their position. His force was just the 1st and 3rd battalions of the Natal Native Infantry. All they could do was 'get on top of a steep hill and make a fort … and we have had such a scare that we have not stopped digging yet'.[7]

Sack and his men were clearly isolated. The picture we have here is of the sheer vulnerability of all scattered forces after the defeat. Sack's men, he said, 'have such a holy fear of Zulus that if there is an alarm, which happens regularly twice or three times a week, they all bolt in every direction and it takes a day to get them together again'. There was no communication and no information brought to them, wherever they were positioned. Sack did not know where he was. He wrote to his father 'I don't put my address because the place has no name but it is somewhere on the frontier about 30 miles from a beastly little place called Greytown.'[8]

All that could be done, in between the alarms, was drill. He noted, 'We have about 200 kaffirs and 60–70 whites – about 30 mounted. As to the weapons: some of the natives had Martini-Henrys and some had Sniders or Enfields, but mostly they had assegais and knobkerries.' Sack's account of drill is done humorously, but it throws light on the amateurism and sheer mess of the forces behind the imperial infantry, engineers and so on who had gone on to fight:

> The men with firearms go in the skirmish line and the assegai men form the reserve and when close enough to the supposed enemy are made to charge. It is the queerest charge imaginable … they run as fast as you can gallop and yell like mad and the ground is very steep and full of holes so some of them go over and over them, the niggers yell, the sergeants swear and all the horses bolt and altogether it takes about an hour to get the regiment together. Hardly any of us speak Kaffir ...[9]

In plain terms, this sheds light on the nature of the preparations Chelmsford and Frere had existing behind the main lines. Of course, the three columns sent forward and the two columns in reserve at crucial points of protection and communication were seemingly intelligently planned, and Chelmsford knew the priorities, but what Sack Lane-Fox's letters home show is that in a large number of auxiliaries (and this was a war of second-liners and late arrivals) there was chaos and very little knowledge of the enemy. 'Hardly any of us speaks Kaffir' was something Wolseley would not have allowed.

Communication was hearsay. Sack notes that 'They say' that there was a naval brigade two hundred and fifty strong coming up along the bank and two companies of the 14th coming from Maritzburg. Sack saw the reality of the situation: 'If we move anywhere by ourselves we must be smashed.' We have an insight into the terrain also when he notes that 'If the river goes down a little lower … the Zulus will cross and look us up.' All they could do was sit and wait, under arms every morning, from half past two. It rained most of the time and there was a mist. Sack noted that 'The sun comes out and takes all the skin off your hands and face and then sets fire to the grass.'[10]

He soon wanted out of all that, writing to his father asking to get him leave 'even if it means resignation in my name'. He never saw a Zulu, and he died from dysentery in Durban on 28 August. His mother wrote to him, 'It is a great disappointment to us that you never 8 [sic] Zulu'. The last report on him was that 'he was very patient and brave to the last. He passed away without any effort or struggle …'[11]

Sack's father had pulled all the strings he could to get his son out to Natal. In September 1877 he had asked Willoughby Loudon to help, and his friend replied, 'What is to be done about Bay [another nickname given to Sack] – all the foreign applications seem to have fallen through. Lady Conyers has had no answer from Colonel Roberts.'[12]

ARTHUR HENRY SALTMARSHE, D. CIRCA JUNE 1878

Saltmarshe was involved in the Kaffir War – the 9th Cape Frontier War – and was on his way to Natal when he died. We do not know precisely how and where he died, but his brief story informs us of other matters concerning the preparation for war against the Zulu.

On 3 April 1878 he was at Fort Beaufort, Cape of Good Hope, and he reported home that there had been some fighting 'down in the Pirie bush'. He borrowed a rifle from his Uncle Arthur, who was on his way home. But he was soon close to danger. He was attached to the 90th (Perthshire) Light Infantry and with him was Robert Hackett, who was to be prominent in the Khambula attack a year later with Evelyn Wood.

Men of the 24th Regiment were also with Saltmarshe, so he was in the thick of the action. He recalled that Hackett had a close encounter: 'One of our officers, Major Hackett, had rather a narrow escape the other night. He was visiting a guard close to the camp when an assegai whizzed close to his shoulder – this is the way these kaffirs do it if they get a chance at a single or even 2 or 3 men …'[13] Saltmarshe had sailed on the *Nubian* in late February and was marching almost as soon as he landed, as he wrote to his father: 'Three columns from here start almost at once, my own company with 2 guns ... the whole, under Stevens, start tonight.' He was then at King Williams Town and wrote of the Zulu, thinking he was being sent on to join the Chelmsford force there, 'Opinions differ about the war, some think it won't last long as the niggers have very little to eat … in fact they say there is to be a famine in that part of the country …'[14]

But Arthur died, and Colonel Cherry-Garrard wrote to Saltmarshe's father that there had been an encounter with the enemy as they were heading towards Pietermaritzburg. His regiment was walking the 500 miles from King Williams Town. He wrote, 'We went in order to settle the Zulu War and we cannot do anything but sell the bulk of the things at once.' He meant the belongings of Arthur Saltmarshe. There had been an attack and the officer explained: 'Stevens has recovered wonderfully though the bullet has not been extracted in spite of several operations at the base of his brain ... I'm sorry to say that 2 or 3 of the wounded men died later in the day …'[15] One of those was Arthur.

What does this scrap of evidence from the front tell us? That yet another body of men was going to join Chelmsford, and they were to march 500 miles. They clearly had very little knowledge of the land or the people and they were short of basic equipment – Saltmarshe had to take a relative's rifle.

If we put these two small, marginal narratives together as a prelude to what is to come as a perspective on all types of intelligence in the Zulu War, we find a picture of the gathering army behind the advance as one of disorder, pragmatic arrangements and amateurism. It completes a picture of a colony recently claimed, as Britain had annexed the Transvaal, but little known. An interesting addition to this is to look at the notes made by the novelist H Rider Haggard as he travelled with the diplomat Theophilus Shepstone. Here is a classic template of the gentleman-traveller, the kind of man who would have been recruited by the more enlightened officers when active in the far reaches of the Empire.

Haggard signed up as a volunteer in 1877, and late in that year he met Anthony Trollope, writing home about him: 'He stopped in the country about twelve days, and now is going home to write a book about it … I call such a proceeding dishonesty, making use of a great name to represent a country.' Haggard exemplified perfectly the type of individual who was there in the Transvaal at the time, gathering knowledge of a practical kind. He noted that, as he assessed the Zulu situation, 'It is hoped the Chief [Shepstone] will be able to stave off this Zulu business until April, because the horse sickness would render all cavalry useless at that time of year.'[15]

To sum up, the amateurs, chancers and younger sons in need of a war to make a name mixed with those civilians who on the contrary did have a genuine interest in the peoples and cultures of southern Africa. What we learn from looking at accounts of these people is that, as with the Great Game in India, it was time for the high command to see a place for some of them, a place other than merely helping to swell a regiment, as was the case with Sackville Lane-Fox. Of course their stories are often the anti-climax and the deep irony of failure in war, but reading between the lines it is plain to see that here was a resource for the intelligence arm of the army – something recognized in the East but not yet in Africa.

2

Intelligence Establishment in the 1870s

In the 1830s in Britain, society was consolidating its quest for applying knowledge of all kinds to the world beyond its shores. The eighteenth-century Enlightenment was beginning to percolate into practical knowledge and the gentleman-scholar was increasingly showing an interest in applying knowledge instead of merely gathering facts and filling notebooks with description and analysis. Yet paradoxically, the new towns of the Industrial Revolution still reflected the persistence of marginal and pseudo-scientific occupations such as astrologers, 'wise women' and so-called 'cunning folk'. The sharpest contrast is perhaps to note that while ordinary working people were visiting cunning folk to ask about illness or future work, science was giving forensics the Marsh test to identify arsenic traces in suspected poisoning cases.

The Society for the Diffusion of Useful Knowledge reflects this interest in moving away from folk tales and superstition to practical knowledge in its 1828 publication *The British Almanac*. As Roy Porter notes, 'From that hour it was piously declared, the empire of astrology was at an end.'[17] Every new profession (and many of the old ones) was starting the long process of modernizing attitudes and attempting to gather knowledge of all kinds. The Royal Geographical Society was founded in 1830 and its importance for future military intelligence can be observed in its relationship to David Livingstone: although his interests were missionary rather than military, it is notable that when he began his trek to find Lake Ngami in 1849 and he had to cross the Kalahari Desert, his achievement typified what was increasingly going on in the ranks of the political officers in the Raj. As Niall Ferguson puts it: 'The expeditions to Ngami were the first of a succession of almost superhuman journeys that were to enthral the mid-Victorian imagination.'[18]

Gathering knowledge, as a pursuit in itself, was to affect every area of life. When the high command finally recognized the value of having a database of geographical information, the practice of intelligence was transformed. However, in a strange and haphazard manner, the collection of information, even by men working within the East India Company or the British army itself, was rarely collected and used in any purposeful way. As research by Douglas M Peers has shown, scholars within the army treated their information-gathering as something marginal and incidental to their everyday military work. Peers says,

> Military officers and surgeons played a critical role in the collection, analysis and dissemination of knowledge in colonial India. Yet the little attention to date [2005] that has been directed at scholars with military backgrounds has treated their army service as incidental to, rather than formative of, their contributions to knowledge of India.[19]

We are considering a gentlemanly army of scholar-officers here: travel gave them the incentive they craved to play a small part in the new utilitarian world of information. Peers makes the point that many had a primary interest simply in cultural topics, but areas such as linguistic study would naturally prove to be invaluable as the army began to see the need for proper training when political work was undertaken. Before this was acknowledged, men like James Abbott who began their long journeys into the dangerous frontiers in the mountains had somehow taught themselves other languages, and it could prove a perilous amateur endeavour, as Abbott notes in his journey to Khiva. In the course of that epic adventure he had to try to get by with some Arabic, Persian and Hindi.

Naturally, these gentlemen-officers would record, in writing and with drawings, their travels to all corners of the Indian sub-continent and indeed elsewhere in the Empire. But as Peers notes, this information was of mixed value to the army establishment: 'Such local depictions ranged from the banal and anecdotal to detailed and systematic descriptions of local topography and resources.'[20]Arguably the most significant achievement of these men was the creation of their own information networks. On an everyday level it would work in this way: an officer would be posted from one place to another, perhaps from Africa to the Indian frontier; he might be changing from a confrontation with Zulu peoples to Sikhs and Pathans. The climate, culture, languages and military structures would all be different. But the network would be working all the time, in many ways, from journals to newspapers and private letters. Officers would spend months together when they were at home on leave (periods of a year were sometimes spent at home). In the case of India, these men were partly smitten with the 'romance' of the east, of Orientalism, and there was always an element of seeing that world through rose-coloured spectacles. But the hard experience of the Mutiny and of the earlier Sikh Wars would put that right.

This communication network, on which so much of the valuable intelligence was to depend, found consolidation in the establishment of clubs and societies across India. As Peers explains, 'By the third decade of the nineteenth century, officers in India had their own trade periodicals and book clubs ... The membership roll of the Bengal Club, founded in 1828, is replete with military officers: its founding president was General Combermere, commander in chief in India.'[21] After this came the Madras Club in 1831, the Byculla Club in 1833 and the Western India Turf Club in 1837. Some officers within this context made a significant contribution to the baseline knowledge of the culture in which the wars of the Raj were fought. Such a man was Robert Orme, who worked for the East India Company, and his chronicle of military actions in India led to his being appointed the official historiographer of the Company. Orme's accounts of conflicts led to a series of supposed insights (largely generalizations) that would influence major figures in the course of the Raj's history. Comments such as this typify his writing: 'The Hindus have from time to time immemorial been as addicted to commerce, as they are averse to war. They have therefore always been immensely rich and have always been incapable of defending themselves.'[22]

It cannot be denied that from the early nineteenth century, when police informers and *agents provocateurs* were profitably employed by Lord Sidmouth to root out radicals in the working-class movements, to the Crimean War in 1853–1856, all varieties of intelligence gathering were rather ad hoc and rarely well organized. The foundation of the police force in 1830 by Sir Robert Peel was seen by many as the first step towards a totalitarian regime in Britain, but no one in the establishment had complained when some of Feargus O'Connor's 'Physical Force' Chartists were spied upon and monitored as they drilled on Woodhouse Moor in Leeds.

Throughout the century there was an overlap between military intelligence in the strict sense and all foreign affairs. There was also a blurring of distinctions when it came to understanding what the separate roles of the police were, as opposed to the army personnel, when the Fenians and Anarchists began to infiltrate London from the 1850s onwards. In fact, in much popular writing, police spies were seen as the lowest of the low, often depicted melodramatically as if they were products of the worst excesses of the French Revolution.

But the fact remains that from Waterloo to the Crimea, intelligence available to military commanders was often nothing more than hearsay given by travellers or even newspaper articles. Wellington was asked in 1851 about the Kaffir War, and he replied that he had never had any information on the causes of the war, or the objects of the government in carrying it on. The Duke relied on newspaper reports during the period of his last years as commander in chief, 1842–1852.

Another reason why the subject has not been explored for some time is that the army tended to rely on the reports of English gentlemen who travelled in the dangerous regions where border disputes and potential invasions were always likely. The obvious example is Afghanistan, in the period from circa 1830 to the end of the century. Most of the intelligence work when the Russians were seriously engaged in making incursions into India by way of Khiva and Bokhara was done by bold individuals, either private citizens or young officers out to make a reputation.

In many instances, commanders of British forces would be learning desperately important information as they moved their forces around, hoping that the right characters would be on hand, or that sheer courage and reputation would see them through. One of the direst learning experiences was to be in the Zulu campaigns of 1879, when certain examples of the superiority of the intelligence gained by some of the Zulu *impis* shamed the British forces, with their reputation for efficiency.

A typical example of the kind of wayward character who tended to figure prominently in intelligence gathering at the time was Charles Masson, a wanderer and scholar who actually travelled on foot across vast areas of Central Asia, and who was only found out after many years of random information sourcing by Captain Claude Wade, political agent in Ludhiana. Masson was in reality a deserter from the East India Company called James Lewis. While Lieutenant Alexander Burnes had been cultivating the friendship of Dost Mohammad in Kabul, to maintain a buffer state against Russian designs on northern India, Masson/Lewis had been busy also. When the British government wrote to Dost Mohammad in a tone of haughty disapproval, with no real promises made about backing or support for him in military terms, it emerged that Burnes's spying and intelligence-gathering had been in vain: the Russians had been in touch with Dost first and alliances made. Masson blamed Burnes.

The affair highlights the failures and dangers of the methods at work at that time: it was desultory and pragmatic. If information was needed, a young officer would be sent to sort it out. The officers in question usually had command of several languages, had diplomatic skills, and preferably had a talent for making rough maps and accurate sketches as they moved along through potentially hostile people and terrain.

When some kind of system did appear on the table for discussion, it came from a man who was a mere retired major from the Bombay Sappers and Miners. This was Thomas Best Jervis. He had a passion for maps, and worked energetically to persuade the War Office that cartography should be more highly prized. In 1837 he was made Surveyor-General of India, supposed to succeed Colonel Everest, but he became tired of waiting for the chance and came home. There he followed all kinds of practical geography and wrote to Lord Aberdeen to insist that cartography would have helped immeasurably in recent foreign skirmishes.

It took the Crimean War to make heads turn and start listening to Jervis. Lord Raglan, in command of the expedition, was known to comment on his lack of any knowledge of the theatre of war he was about to enter. Amazingly, Jervis obtained a detailed map of the Crimea from a contact in Belgium who found him a map made by the Russian general staff. Jervis was going to be listened to after that. In 1855, the War Office eventually created a specific department for cartography and statistics. Topographical and Statistical (T&S) was to be the first real step towards proper military intelligence within the military establishment.

It has to be asked, however, what kind of intelligence was going to be needed as the Empire expanded and British forces were continually packing up and setting off for distant shores? Clearly, accurate maps were useful, and so was general information about the cultures of the societies who would be hosting our military presence. But what about actual military policy, with some kind of system? In that respect, Britain had learned a hard lesson, and that was from the Prussian Wilhelm Stieber. When he came to the Great Exhibition in 1851, Stieber was seen by many as a 'freelancer', and that instead of being dedicated to the Prussian services, he was in the pay of Russia. It became clear that Stieber had succeeded in operating as a double agent in many European cities, and when he finally surfaced in Russia after some years of absence, he eventually became the man who did most to initiate the feared *Ochrana*, the Russian secret police in the Tsarist empire.

It had to be considered: if other powers could do this kind of covert work, why not Britain? Indeed, we were to learn that aspect of the Great Game in such figures as Major Henri Le Caron, otherwise known as Thomas Beach from Colchester. Yet still it took twenty years from the creation of the T&S to the first formation of the Intelligence Branch. By that time, it was beginning to dawn on the leaders of the armed forces that military intelligence was a much more complex process than had previously been thought. As John Keegan points out in his book *Intelligence in War*, the process involves acquisition, delivery, acceptance, interpretation and implementation. It was surely with a sense of shock and alarm that the commanding officers who controlled the British Empire when the Thukela garrison in the Zulu War Eshowe Campaign of 1879 was ready to move that the Zulus were aware of their intentions. The journal of Lieutenant Hamilton at that time notes that some Zulu spies were captured and gave Colonel Pearson all kinds of startling information, including the fact that the British force was surrounded by 35,000 men. Obviously, the Zulu had a full understanding of the five stages of intelligence: they had acquired knowledge of the garrison, delivered that information to the *impi* generals, accepted the facts as true by observation, interpreted the facts and details in the light of what could be seen and counted, and finally implemented their strategy in response by gathering three *impis* at the right place.

Of course, in 1873, the Intelligence Branch had a massive brief and a whole third of the earth to handle at its province, rather than a stretch of Natal. It seems odd now to read that the first staffing arrangements for the new branch involved, for instance, two officers and a clerk to cover the Russian empire. The base they operated from consisted of a house in Adelphi Terrace and a shambling old coach-house and stables tucked away in Whitehall. The first thought was to provide an office and a name. The rest was assumed to follow as a matter of course. The aims of the new branch were expressed in terms of the preparation of information relating to the military defence of the Empire and the strategical considerations of schemes of defence; the collection and distribution of all information relating to the military geography, resources and armed forces of foreign countries and the British colonies and possessions; the compilation of maps and the translations of documents. The two officers and the clerk must have contemplated the map of Russia with a sense of awe and confusion. They did not consider Africa very much at all. The Army of India and the threat of Russia were of paramount importance. With the knowledge of hindsight, it appears to be the ultimate in short-sightedness to concentrate solely on producing masses of information on the East at the expense of the African continent. But circa 1870 there was so much perceived threat from

Russia, much of this stemming from the reorganization of the Russian officer-class after the reforms in the army subsequent to the abolition of serfdom in 1861, that the British Forward thinkers (Frere being one of them) were affected by a blindness with regard to Africa – at the time seen merely as a colonist centre to be held rather than totally controlled.

In Asia, the backbone of intelligence work had been done by political officers. As far back as 1809 an officer, Captain N P Grant, was sent to Persia with a brief of discovering whether or not it would be possible for a French or a Russian army to reach Karachi via the Persian Gulf. Spying was done in areas such as Baluchistan and in the further reaches of the Punjab by political officers long before there was an Intelligence Branch and before men like Robertson began compiling gazetteers. The officers of the British army who were defined as political officers ranged widely over Asia, looking at resources and topography, assessing the potential enemies and their approaches to warfare. These men travelled in disguise, acting their roles and mixing with the tribesmen who were on the route. The reasons for these covert operations were that such measures were the only methods of gathering knowledge of the enemy. Cetshwayo's Zulu armies, having had methods of spying entrenched in their modus operandi since the days of Shaka, did fairly similar activities. But the political officers were not active in this way in southern Africa in 1879.

There was another factor in the development of political officers in India: they were gathered around charismatic leaders, as a rule. The classic template is the case of Henry Lawrence, who had a coterie around him known as his 'young men'. These were officers in the Indian Political Service – an elite taken from the cream of the crop in both the Indian Civil Service and the Indian Army. There was no equivalent in Natal. Ultimately, of course, the Indian front was really developed on the assumption that the real war was with Russia, so there was a belief that ultimately, after the spying and the adventures in dangerous frontier country, there would be a European-style battle or two. That never really materialized, and so a combination of small wars in the buffer states and frustrating diplomacy went on relentlessly while the intelligence gathering continued merely as a series of ploys to pre-empt Russian expansion eastwards.

All this is absent from South Africa and the reasons for the difference are obvious, the central contrast being that in Africa there was no monolithic oppositional nation or culture to provide a genuine and profound long-term military sense of purpose and even destiny – the imperial theme of Victoria's strong industrialized nation, of course. In one sense it is a contrast of frontiers also. Although the Natal–Zululand border was a frontier, that is to say land that could possibly be contested, it was policed and controlled by magistrates and residents; settlers and native contingents knew it all well. In Asia there were no-go areas and a far more complex interweaving of tribal land and allegiances.

For all these reasons, although a glance at the situation in India is instructive and enlightening, there are limits to the benefits of comparison. That is, in a military sense: there is much more potential in the Eastern political and military map when we come to look at diplomacy within the great imperial machine and the foreign policies emanating from the 'scramble for Africa'. It is also difficult to miss the importance of commanders and their personalities. Although the Indian situation had its Isandlwana in the 1842 retreat from Kabul – a massive disaster with immense loss of life – it was a failure within a pattern, and that pattern was defined and continued by strong, individual personalities. Chelmsford was an old-fashioned soldier who put planning and organization first, before character and dash. In his worldview, military intelligence in both its theoretical and its charismatic form (as exemplified by men such as Sir Richard Burton who travelled into dangerous places and became 'native' on most occasions) was something that was integrated into a master plan. In the actions of the Anglo-Zulu War we can see in Evelyn Wood and Redvers Buller the kind of sparkle and verve that was seen in the earlier heroes of the Great Game in Asia, but they were moving within a firmly designed theatre of war, moves made as in chess, and with the relentless application of tried and tested methods in the field. Of course spying and scouting meant undergoing the kinds of risks associated with the Great Game spies, but it tended to be piecemeal, the result of spontaneous reaction and ad hoc decisions. With that in mind, several of the instances of personal courage in the Zululand campaigns come out as highly outstanding and in many cases unique, as in Rorke's Drift. It is hard to introduce any meaningful comparison with that stunning piece of defensive obduracy and valour in any context.

The intelligence establishment immediately before Lord Chelmsford's columns advanced into Zululand, then, was newly conceived, still seen as rather marginal, and composed of a few specialists: men who were in some ways in advance of their time, like Robertson and Brackenbury. The member of Chelmsford's staff who notably fits in well with those officers was Cornelius Clery, whom *The Times* called 'a military dandy of the old school'.

As previous writers have noted, the intelligence establishment in 1873 was at the very small and tentative doorstep of what would eventually become the great mansion of MI5 and the Intelligence Branch of the army by the first years of the twentieth century. It was no more than an incipient idea, with a base in the field that was still a mixture of skills from sappers, scouts, signallers and riders from cavalry units.

On the broader international stage, the subject of confederation lies behind much of what happened in Zululand. In Disraeli's government, Lord Carnarvon had settled Canada as a confederation, and so he reasoned that such an arrangement would be useful in southern Africa, as there were various settlers, most prominently the Boers. Carnarvon sent out the historian J A Froude on two visits in 1874 and 1875, with the brief of lecturing on the benefits of confederation. A projected conference on the subject in London then failed to achieve anything. Disraeli was disenchanted, but then, after the Boers were beaten by Sekukuni of the Bapedi tribe, there was pressure to try again, and Carnarvon saw that the Transvaal was the first stepping-stone towards confederation. He sent Shepstone to effect annexation, and it was Carnarvon who appointed Sir Bartle Frere as High Commissioner for southern Africa. After that, any diplomacy that might be geared towards links with intelligence work (which again tended to happen in India) was never going to happen.

Disraeli, too preoccupied with other foreign issues such as Afghanistan, took a back seat and let Carnarvon go to work.

The result was that, taking a wider picture of the development of military intelligence at this time, matters of information and liaison with native peoples was left to educated and experienced amateurs – gentlemen administrators who were not at all the same as political officers appointed within the ranks of the army.

If the following narrative appears to praise Sir Garnet Wolseley rather too much, then that is because at the very time that the new office was opened for intelligence staff in London he was fighting the Ashanti with as much brain as brawn, and he saw the need for intellectual, learned officers who saw the use of having information about the enemy to hand when required. Although he arrived after the central confrontations of the war, and with Chelmsford triumphant after Ulundi and the capture of Cetshwayo, he still represents the attitudes to all aspects of intelligence work which were going to become standard, although that was to take another twenty years to accomplish. Wolseley has come to represent that breed of officer who, in spite of a certain reputation for arrogance and back-biting, got things done. He had the charisma, and of course he invariably delivered the results. His letters to his friend Sir John Maurice, in later life, reveal that side of his character which perhaps relied too much on adulation and evident, clearly demonstrated respect, but as with Kitchener and Buller, to a large extent that was the right attitude in that time and in that place.

3

Diplomats and Border Agents: The Prelude

Military intelligence is basically about knowledge of the enemy. That sounds very simple, but of course a reflection on the nature of 'knowledge' soon leads to complex questions about partiality, trust, responsibility and above all the status and source of the knowledge. This applies in all areas of human activity, but in war, it applies in terms of saving lives, preserving reputations and even at times ensuring the progress of a great ideological machine called an empire.

For Victorian commanders, confronted with a variety of enemy forces each with their own weapons, tactics and shared aims, often with tribal loyalties and various bonds of allegiance through kinship, there was a base-line body of knowledge relating to the foundations of military thinking required. In the case of the Zulu kingdom, the back-story was well known, as the fame of Shaka, founder of the modern military systems of the nation, was widely known beyond Africa. In a large number of periodicals and ephemera from the Regency period to the 1860s there was a burgeoning of interest in the 'Dark Continent' and indeed all other corners of the world. A typical issue of *Home Friend* for example, published in 1857, just after the Crimean War, contained, for general readership, an account of the Zouave warriors, a tract on 'Field Fortification and Siege Work' and a piece on the Walcheren expedition. Military affairs naturally interested the reading public when so many of them had relatives abroad, fighting in all the little wars of Victoria's reign as well as in the major conflicts.

However, the information that really mattered was the mix of the current intelligence and fundamental knowledge. That combination meant that it would be possible to predict the enemy actions. Again, everyone seemed to have an opinion on this and, once more, Rider Haggard had a theory in his head: 'I think I told you that their plan of battle is to engage us in the open for three days and three nights and then charge in from every side.'[23] He had been told about the Zulu 'horns of the buffalo' tactic. Clearly, Shepstone was his teacher, and this opens up the whole subject of the diplomats and the border agents in the period before Chelmsford's advance north.

The men already in place, men such as Shepstone, knew the country, but they were not there to prepare maps, and maps were, naturally, a key element in the essential knowledge on which intelligence in the field could work. As discussed in the previous chapter, Thomas Best Jervis had seen the importance of cartography, but even by the 1870s it was not a priority. Henry Curling notes the problem, writing in 1878: 'The lack of accurate maps was a handicap during the invasion of Zululand and great reliance was placed on the colonial scouts to seek out the best routes. The Royal Engineers took the opportunity to survey and produce the first accurate maps of the region.'

Shepstone, knowledgeable as he was on Zulu civilization, was war-mongering with Bartle Frere: he told Frere in January 1878 that no peace was possible until the Zulu power was crushed. Everything began to focus on the Boundary Commission, which started to consider the situation with regard to the three main interests in Zululand – Zulu, British and Boer. The Commission met on 12 March 1878 at Rorke's Drift, but the expected outcome, that the Boers would be given their share and there would be a war, was not so straightforward. One reason was that the Colonial Secretary, Carnarvon, was replaced by Sir Michael Hicks Beach. He did not have the same set opinions as Frere, so there was to be more debate. Hicks Beach was more open to consider the Zulu position, and so what becomes particularly interesting with regard to the gathering of intelligence on the Zulu is the correspondence between John

Sutcliffe Robson, Eustace Fannin, border agents at Umvoti, together with magistrates Henry Fynn junior and W H Beaumont, and Hicks Beach.

Robson, born in 1824, had sailed for Natal from Gravesend in 1850, and settled at Newcastle, Natal. There he became a JP and was a special border agent. When war broke out he went with the Newcastle Buffalo Border Guard, a force of only twenty men when first formed. They were sent with the Centre Column in the advance into Zululand and eventually joined Durnford at Isandlwana, standing with him at the last. The various volunteer groups were essential to Chelmsford: he had only an inadequate force of imperial soldiers, and in order to create the advance he wanted he desperately needed native volunteers. Almost 300 volunteers were to take part in the campaign. Obviously, people such as Robson were immensely valuable for intelligence, and his messages to Hicks Beach illustrate the potential knowledge and local information at the disposal of the high command.

Fynn was born in the Cape Colony in 1846 and became a magistrate in Msinga after working with Shepstone; he was the interpreter at the meeting when the British ultimatum was given and later, as the advance was close at hand, Chelmsford drafted in Fynn to be a special intelligence adviser. He had been with Chelmsford at Mangeni when Isandlwana took place. He figures prominently in Chelmsford's planning in transit as well as before the move north. Fannin was particularly effective in enrolling police, so that groups were speedily assembled to watch key points on the Tugela river.

Chelmsford had been given permission by Sir Henry Bulwer to raise 7,000 native troops in November 1878, and not long before Christmas after that the Boundary Commission was in favour of the Zulus, but the thirteen conditional clauses included what amounted to a direct provocation to war. Therefore, as Cetshwayo was told to disband his army and accept a British resident at Ulundi, war was coming soon. Between December and January, just before the battle of Isandlwana, Robson wrote from Ulundi with his reports for Hicks Beach. Parallel with this, Chelmsford was writing to Evelyn Wood and others, explaining his thinking and planning. The gap between the two is very informative about the difference between actually working to understand the Zulu and their homeland, and the military preparations: it is a case of Chelmsford meticulously working out and anticipating moves, responses and problems, while Hicks Beach gets solid facts.

The intelligence reports concern attitudes among the Zulu, movements, hints about whether or not Cetshwayo was preparing for war, and constantly there are comments on the river, as waiting for the level to decrease was crucial to the advance of Chelmsford's columns. From 1 January to the day of Isandlwana, the reports came to Hicks Beach and of course then to Chelmsford, up to the point of departure. What then becomes apparent is how the important information given in the days preceding the disastrous rout was used or passed on.

Fannin was at Umvoti, and there he spoke to any stray Zulu with scraps of information and placed men by the river on watch. On 1 January he listed possibilities, based on his conjectures of likely developments:

> The men of the tribes might simply be ordered to take their stand along the river and resist any attempt at an inroad, sending instant intelligence to me by way of the police. They might take up their quarters at their kraals of the respective tribes which were nearest …[24]

Robson also had a string of spies out on watch, reporting on 6 January that 'a reliable source' had told him that reinforcements had gathered with Sihayo, an inkosi (hereditary chief) of the iNdabakawombe people, who was based by the mountain Ngedla. Some of his most enlightening statements are drawn from natives who had been travelling across the river: 'This may be only boasting, but it is well known that both the tribe of Sihayo and that of Matyana are burning to try their strength with the English. Large parties of mounted and armed Zulus may be seen riding from point to point.'[25]

The information was flowing in, but what we learn from this is that, with Zululand being 10,450 square miles and Ulundi (the main objective of Chelmsford's drive north) far to the north-east, communication had to be efficient. Even between Frere and Henry Bulwer there was confusion and a certain amount of nervousness, as can be seen in this exchange:

> January 7 1879
>
> I conclude this kind of information is regularly communicated direct by the border officials to the officers in the military detachments.
>
> H. B. E. Frere
>
> Colonial Secretary,
>
> I think you have given instructions to all the border agents to communicate with the officer commanding the nearest column.
>
> H. Bulwer[26]

Such notes convey a sense of anxiety, of giving additional reminders and sometimes rather fretful statements as if the communication system was not regarded with confidence. In practical terms, as Chelmsford was sending three columns north – one from the lower drift, Chelmsford's own, going from Rorke's Drift, and a third from the headwaters of the Blood River – it meant that the border police and reserve personnel who were being hurriedly recruited by Fannin and Robson would have to be prepared to cover large distances and move very speedily. Instructions were issued and sent to Robson:

> **Instructions for Native Border Police**
>
> **General Duties** – The general duties of the Border Police will be to watch the fords, to gather intelligence, and to ascertain the business of all natives crossing from either side.
>
> **Directions, Stations** – They will be stationed in such places as the Border Agent of the district shall from time to time direct.
>
> Conveying intelligence – The Border Agent will make his own arrangements as to the method of conveying intelligence by the Police to himself. He will transmit all intelligence that he considers deserving of credit or of any significance to the

> Colonial Secretary, for the information of the Lieutenant-Governor and to the officer in command of the military line in which his district is, using special messengers to such convenient points when the matter to be communicated is of urgent importance.[27]

What was happening was something that had been well established in India for over a century: the liaison between regional magistrates and the army. It was by a magistrate that the *thuggee* killers had been apprehended, using spies to infiltrate gangs. In Zululand, men like Robson were magistrates also: he lived in a small fortress, in effect. His home had a jail and he had servants and police. As a settler, he represented a kind of law and administration that the Zulu would have found very strange, but they would have seen his power and respected it.

Now Robson, Fannin and others were to act as effectively the only intelligence arm of Chelmsford's force outside his official ranks. Because the field intelligence had always been undertaken, since Wellington's days in particular, by a mix of scouting detachments, Royal Engineers and adjutants with power to select individuals, the plan of having three columns appears on paper to be sensible: it meant that detachments of scouts could move quickly and meet any riders from the Border Police. But there was one major obstacle: the country itself. The topography was such that with the deep-cut valleys, the dongas and the sheer number of undulations of all kinds, communications were always going to be problematical, and were to prove fatal at Isandlwana

The information kept pouring in from Fannin and Robson in January. Fannin was recruiting new police, and his notes imply that he was being given provisions, as he had badges delivered on 2 January. But he needed greatcoats for them 'to render them efficient in wet weather'. He was probably asking for funds.

On 5 January the Tugela was still too high to cross. But Fannin's police reported regularly that there were Zulu across the river, eager to fight. What then began to be included in the reports was something more than facts. Intelligence reports always need a dimension other than the facts, though they are something to be considered and often wrong. What started to happen was that assessments were made of intangible elements, such as can be seen in this statement:

> I think I am justified in saying that there is a better feeling growing up among our own natives. I think they have more confidence in our power to overcome the Zulus, and see that, to use a common expression, they are in the same boat, and must sink or swim with us.[28]

There were also the usual ruses. After all, what was Cetshwayo doing while these preparations were in progress? He was a master of misinformation, just as in the field the Zulu habit was a feint and the use of deception, so there were various stories given to civilians, such as the reports from Bishop Schroeder at the Christian mission in Robson's area. The Bishop said that Cetshwayo had given orders for all the younger warriors to go to him at Ulundi, and that only the older men were along the river, to reduce the chance of a clash with the guards and police. This may have been true, but it is likely that this was a temporary measure, preparatory to the King sorting out which *impis* would be deployed in specific locations. In other words, the informants who told Schroeder to put another 'spin' on the story.

However, Fannin and Robson had trusted men, and these were sent as spies into Zululand. On 11 January Fannin wrote to describe a spy sent twenty miles beyond the Tukanhla forest, so he would have been in the heart of the southern area of Zululand. The spy was smart enough to note minor but telling details such as this: 'My informant took note of one very significant act of the Zulus. Two very old men, named Manxondo and Bilibana, who live near the Tugela and who are unable to walk, have this week been carried away on men's shoulders to kraals on the edge of the Inkhanla forest for safety.' These were not just any random Zulu people: Manxondo was a tribal chief and Bilbana was a highly rated warrior.[29]

Other spies reported, just two days later, that John Dunn's place, Emangeto, was then crowded with gathering warriors. John Dunn (who is to figure in chapter 6) was to become a very important figure in the intelligence within Chelmsford's army, notably later, in the aftermath of the setback at Isandlwana. He had lived among the Zulu for many years and so he was extremely valuable to the British when he 'came across', and he had already requested, before the Zulu arrived at his home, that his family and servants be given somewhere to stay in Natal. They had been dealt with by Henry Bulwer, who had advised that the people be used in the Public Works Department, and very meanly he remarked that as Dunn was a rich man he need not ask the British government to feed the employees.

Fannin's spies gave details of a more precise nature by 15 January. But on 11 January, Chelmsford's Centre Column was crossing the river at Rorke's Drift. It is hardly surprising that Fannin reported that one of his contacts reported in Zululand, 'two Zulu doctors were daily expected to sprinkle for war all the tribes living near this border'.

All this shows just how important the magistrates were in the context of intelligence. Foremost in many ways was Henry Fynn Junior, who had been with Shepstone and Haggard when Cetshwayo was 'crowned' – a meaningless ceremony in which there was a proclamation of peace with regard to Zululand and its neighbours. Fynn became a very important interpreter, and after Isandlwana he played an important role in setting up border guards. He had also helped Chelmsford in the diplomacy involved in meeting Gamdana, a brother of Sirayo.

Is it clear from some of Chelmsford's letters from camp, though, that he had treated the reports from border agents with scepticism. On 21 January he wrote to Bartle Frere: 'I do not believe Mr Fannin's report about a large force in the Inkandla bush, and I am certain that the Tugela river at the present moment is not one which a force would dare to dash across. Middledrift moreover is still watched by two battalions of Col. Durnford's column.' Yet Fannin and Robson had both sent missives when the river level was low enough to cross. Up-to-date information was crucially important, as is surely seen in the statement by Frere that a large portion of the regiments' warriors would be harvesting grain at the time of the advance – something proved wrong when it was noted that the rains were later than expected.

The diplomats, from Shepstone and Fynn down to the local magistrates, were extremely important in the initial phase of intelligence gathering, and of course they were also recruiting police. There were also the native contingents, as already noted. Shepstone was particularly important; he had become so familiar to the Zulu that they had a nickname for him – 'Sompseu', meaning 'mighty hunter'. He could speak with confidence and intimate knowledge of the Zulu culture, tradition and language. Men like him and the other settlers who played these major roles in intelligence were self-made: they learned by doing. When Rider Haggard was appointed Master and Registrar of the High Court in May 1877 he had no legal training at all. Yet he learned and coped well. As for Shepstone, he had been agent for the native tribes since 1845. At a time when fluent speakers of Zulu were in short supply, he, together with Fynn, were arguably the key figures in establishing information sources, despite the fact that Shepstone wanted what Frere wanted, and had the utter assurance that he was right. The attitudes of the imperialists such as he are expressed succinctly in a publication of twenty years after the wars – a geography of the Empire from 1899, which has these words: 'The Zulu king was reinstated in 1883, but died the following year and the British government, finding that the Zulus could not form any orderly government, declared the country British territory in 1887.'

Although the settlers and diplomats were part of the scene in the intelligence establishment, they were often led by personal vision and the imperial ideologies they embraced thoughtlessly, and of course the paternalistic attitudes to African people did little to improve their status when it came to their approaches and thoughts being tested by change and warfare.

After all this, it was the turn for field intelligence and communication to take centre stage. Reading Chelmsford's papers today, what strikes us is the fundamental habit of thought which John Laband describes: 'it is hardly surprising that field intelligence under Chelmsford during the Anglo-Zulu War was minimal. He had no intelligence officer on his staff in January 1879 and he saw no need for such an appointment.'[30] In December 1878 he wanted someone to act as intelligence officer, but Cornelius Clery, who was interested in tactics and theory, had been assigned to Colonel Glyn with the Centre Column. There is something disturbingly whimsical and careless in Chelmsford's letter when he says, 'Have you anyone who could take up Clery's work pro tem? I am most anxious to give Glyn a good staff officer before the time arrives for him to move down to Rorke's Drift, and I have absolutely no-one available.'[31] That implies that Clery was the only man suitable for any forward role in field intelligence. Major Clery had served in Griqualand West in 1877 and in the Transvaal in 1878. Interestingly, he had been an instructor in tactics at The Royal Military College, being a professor there in 1872–1875.

The overall picture of intelligence, then, on the eve of Isandlwana, was that the three columns were about to move into Zululand with only border agents ahead, simply watching the river crossings, and settlers who had local knowledge firmly entrenched in their own fastnesses – with the exception of Henry Fynn.

4

Lessons of Isandlwana

Underlying all the foregoing comments on what intelligence there was and what was not available is the fundamental fact that in colonial warfare the Victorian armies were working on improvisation. As the locations of conflicts were so varied and the enemies so assorted in their characteristics, each expeditionary force had to be pragmatic; it was ingrained in commanders that the approach was one of adapt and move one step at a time. Chelmsford was also merely one officer in a massive network across the red areas on the world map. The ideologies at work in Whitehall were by the 1870s dominated by two lines of thought about the Empire: one was for conservation and the other for expansion. The plans and strategies from Chelmsford, Frere and others were in line with the Forward Policy. If war was assumed to be happening, then it would take its course as all previous ones had done – that was the thinking.

Therefore in the small-scale immediate theatre of war in Zululand, officers, men and units were moved around to respond to situations as they arose. Most important of all factors here was the place itself. Some have explained this as 'wars against nature', meaning that what information intelligence really should supply was that body of fact linked to landscape, climate and topography. In Africa, these elements were more daunting than enemy formations; as was noted in the two case studies of young adventurers, the foremost threats were the heat of the sun and bacteria. Every waking moment meant attention to little problems and obstacles stemming from the location. This also affected lines of communication, of course: the naval brigade which arrived and landed on 19 November 1878 did indeed play an active part in several engagements and was used in ferrying men. This was common practice across the Empire: navigable rivers were one of the first considerations in imperial wars.

Perhaps most challenging of all for the imperial armies was the great diversity in enemy tactics. This meant that British approaches were constantly being changed and adapted. Basic thinking was either that a line or a square be applied: after Isandlwana, the square was prioritized. But basic to all was the need to be proactive: wherever the army went, the approach had to be to go and confront the enemy. Nothing really changed the mindset that worked by short moves and immediate consolidation of a position. The reliance was on the solid discipline of the unit overcoming the chaos and disorder of a so-called 'primitive people's' attack mode. While the wars were being fought, the theory was slowly emerging; yet in the failures at Isandlwana, a lesson of mammoth proportions was learned.

With the wisdom of hindsight, it may easily be seen that the fragmentation in such terrain was the cause of the defeat. Sensible arrangements such as the laagering of all wagons when in camp were fine, but when scouting parties failed to gather any definite knowledge of enemy positions and strength, the chips were down. The official report by the Intelligence Branch (of 1880) has a typical example of this: 'Though on the previous day Zulu scouts had been observed on the distant hill tops, none had appeared so close to the British troops and Colonel Pearson now ordered this party to be dispersed by the Natal Native Contingent ... this was done and the scouts all disappeared ...'[32] But then, when a *kloof* (a woody ravine) was crossed to do this, a large body of Zulu were surprisingly observed. The report was, as Ian Knight has explained, largely based on the conclusions of the enquiry set up by Chelmsford at Helpmekaar in February, just after the event. Colonel Arthur Harness was officiating at that enquiry, and it is clear that his brief was to offer an explanation of the failure to defend the position at Isandlwana. Harness, who went to the Frontier War before being sent with the N/5 Battery of the Royal Artillery, had been moving six guns on the fateful day, but the transport was very slow in the resistant terrain; he was ordered to go on when news of the attack came, but never made it there. He was then told to shell the battlefield, probably with the aim of destroying any Zulu there who might be scavenging on bodies.

Harness did not use all of the information given by survivors, and so a partial view emerged. The 1880 report reads in a very reductive, methodical way, as if there is no intention to elaborate, but simply to state a string of facts which would inevitably lead to the condemnation of certain officers and their unwise decisions. That would give Chelmsford a scapegoat or two, of course. The events of 22 January are consequently given as a string of movements and decisions, all in response to Zulu sightings or reports. The focus on Durnford is at the heart of the report's findings: early in the morning of the battle he had orders to move his column (the Second) forwards to Isandlwana, and he arrived there at around ten o'clock. He took over command from Colonel Pulleine and the report notes that there was a disagreement about deployment of companies as responses were made to scouts' reports of Zulu movements. Durnford sent a company back to protect supplies and he then advanced with two companies of the 24th and a company of Natal Native Contingent. The important paragraph in this context, as the first stage of the fragmentation of the British forces happened, is surely this: 'With this he left camp about 11 a.m., and advanced along the plain in front, with the object of preventing the columns of the enemy, reported as in retreat, from joining the force with which Lord Chelmsford was at that time believed to be engaged.'[33] This is all about misinformation – about poor field intelligence and urgent though unthinking responses. Durnford reportedly then sent another company of the 1/24th to check the high ground and there they saw what scouts had already seen – the main Zulu army advancing in line.

What should have been the next move? The Zulu advance, spanning two valleys, was in the traditional buffalo-horn formation and it did not break up to confront small pockets of British who fired on them. The successful tactic was being used again, relentlessly being applied, and the report makes it clear that there was further fragmentation in the British as companies moved out to support small units. In other words, the central force of troops, the ones who would face the 'head' of the buffalo formation, would be depleted. A retreat was ordered so that men could fall back to reinforce the main body. Durnford and his party then also fell back, but were allegedly distracted by another action involving the Basuto soldiers. Of course, the 'horns' of the buffalo in the Zulu formation then began to be seen and confronted, again only by marginal groups who simply reacted in panic.

There were only three companies fighting in the northern area of the battlefield and to the east two companies of the 24th were thinly distributed. What had happened was that no central grasp of the situation had been possible because the Zulu army had come relentlessly and speedily, and had not been seen and understood in time for a planned reaction. As the report makes clear: 'Meanwhile the advance of the Zulus continued steadily. And without check or halt.'[34] From ten past one to around two pm the sequence of events inevitably led to a necessity for courageous last stands against masses of warriors.

It was nine thirty in the morning when Chelmsford received the information that the Zulus were advancing in force from the left of the camp. Yet attempts to see and understand what was happening failed; a view from a telescope brought no knowledge of events, and it was a quarter past one before a messenger from the Natal Native Contingent came with the message from Captain Browne: 'For God's sake come with all your men; the camp is surrounded and will be taken unless helped.' It was much too late for anything to be done. Around noon, first a sergeant and then Captain Devlin rode to try to carry messages on the parlous state of affairs, but these were doomed to failure.

The Intelligence Branch report, then, compiles facts in such a way that there are implications of blame: Durnford is singled out as a man who took decisions rashly. But it is clear from all reports that no one had time for any other kind of decision. The defeat appears, with hindsight, to be a confrontation between a Zulu army which was flexible, able to move quickly and which knew the landscape well, and the British army which did not remain solid and unified, being afraid that field intelligence was not attainable from any one viewpoint.

The latter was the basic reason for fragmentation: so many companies were deployed across a wide area that there were only partial views and scraps of knowledge available, leading to snap decisions. On the other hand, the Zulus could very efficiently send spies into protected positions where they could observe the movement of troops who had to move with noise, problems of topography and only one relentless attitude of seeking out the enemy and forming lines of firepower. One of the most telling details of this comes from Henry Curling's note in his memoirs:

> When we turned out again about 12, the Zulus were only showing on the left of our camp. All the time we were idle in the camp, the Zulus were surrounding us with a huge circle several miles in circumference and hidden by hills from our sight. We none of us felt the least anxious as to the result for, although they came in immense numbers, we felt it impossible that they could break through.[35]

The British had no idea that the huge arc of Zulus was moving, as one horn of the buffalo, and any frontal attack was going to mean a huge numerical disadvantage for the British troops.

The Zulu army, by Ian Knight's estimate, numbered approximately 24,000 men. He makes the point that the leader, Chief Ntshingwayo kaMahole, was a skilled tactician, deeply imbued with the traditions of the Zulu Royal House, a natural leader. In fact, the more we reflect on the nature of the 'horns of the buffalo' tactic – the *izimpondo zankomo* – the more it has to be understood that this leant itself to any terrain. If the force was massive enough, so that a vast area could be covered, then the basic concept was sure to succeed as long as there was numerical advantage. The two horns would arc into the circle to surround the enemy, and the 'body' as the solid part would have the depth to cope with a frontal assault. If the British had combined to make that frontal assault on the body of the 'buffalo' then by attrition, progress would be made, but only if the true strength of the Zulu force were known could there have been any realistic ploy against them in those circumstances.

When Chelmsford voiced his first responses and gave at least one reason for the debacle, it was in a letter to Bartle Frere. He wrote, after learning that the camp was being attacked, 'At that time I had no doubt but that the reported attack was of small importance and that the force in camp would be quite sufficient to beat it off.' He gives no reasons as to why he thought the attack was 'of small importance' and it is hard to see on what evidence he thought that.[36]

In the end, the simple conclusion that the British were 'playing away from home' is a major factor, and even though the imperial armies were accustomed to that situation, this was not the standard imperial army, of course: it was a hotch-potch. The artillery could not be used to optimum effect and the supporting forces, including the native rifles and the naval brigade, were not near enough to know the real situation with regard to the numbers and composition of the Zulu army. Again, comparisons with the Indian Army are tempting: there, the tribesmen the British fought also fought on their own terrain, and they often defeated smaller forces, but on the whole, Britain, with considerable numerical disadvantage, ruled a massive sub-continent by understanding the inner geopolitics and the tendency for Indian peoples to resist any united action. 1857 proved the limitations of that, but even so, the counter attacks were successful because, among other things, the establishment of means of gathering intelligence was more substantial there.

Of all the criticisms potentially to be made against Chelmsford for the disaster at Isandlwana, arguably the dominant one is the lack of any grasp of the real situation with regard to the Zulu army and its nature. In a letter to Colonel Wood on 16 January we see this very clearly. He wrote: 'We must try and push everyone slowly before us towards the King's kraal, or otherwise disarm the tribe and take their chiefs and some of their headmen, as hostages for good behaviour …'[37]It is in Chelmsford's CV that we find reasons for this lack of an authentic engagement with the Zulu context. When he first went to southern Africa he fought the Xhosa, and although he completed the actions against the Gaika in three months, they were not at all like the Zulu, with no formal concept of a military state. It had been more a case of guerrilla tactics against disciplined and hardened troops. Chelmsford's success there (and the subsequent award of the Grand Cross of the Bath) perhaps boosted his self-esteem so much that his over-confidence dominated when his practical grasp of the enemy capability should have been foremost.

The details of the battle of Isandlwana are well known and the events, related to the 1880 report, have been well told by several writers, mainly Ian Knight, Adrian Greaves and Saul David. But in terms of the wider picture of the development of military intelligence, how was it seen and what lessons were learned in that context, particularly in the years immediately after the event? The mediation of the battle in popular culture when compared with military assessments also makes interesting reading.

The political response, which of course was very influential on the more military one, was expressed in Disraeli's letter to the Queen on 11 February:

> It has been a very agitating day with this terrible news from South Africa, which to Lord Beaconsfield is very unintelligible. The Cabinet met and I have sent five regiments of infantry instead of three asked for by Lord Chelmsford, and the cavalry, and artillery and stores which he requested. It is hoped that he may be equal to the occasion but it is impossible not to feel that this disaster has occurred to the Headquarters column which he was himself commanding.[38]

Notwithstanding the Helpmakaar enquiry, the fact was that Disraeli had it just right – it was the commander who was to blame. This clearly had an impact on other reactions.

Archibald Forbes, writing in *The Nineteenth Century* periodical a year after Isandlwana, seized on the obvious errors. He had made his name as a correspondent in the 1877 Russo-Turkish campaign where he had actually been at the centre of things and had contracted a fever. He later went to Cyprus and then to India where he witnessed defences near the Khyber Pass. He rushed from the east after the news from Isandlwana and was there to witness Ulundi. In his essay he wrote, as so many commentators did, on military theory and was (as we shall see in chapter 7), as most correspondents were, a factor in changing views of military intelligence. Regarding the Zulu situation he saw Chelmsford's best move as being an advance from

Utrecht to Ulundi. That would have meant a route from the north-east to the south-west, and he explained it in this way:

> An advance from Utrecht in the direction of Ulundi, athwart the north-eastern region of Zululand, offered the inducements that it would cut off the Zulu retreat into the country of the Swazis, inspire useful confidence in that fighting race, distract the concentration of the Zulu attention on the advance from the south-east, and open up the obscurest parts of the hostile region.[39]

Forbes pointed out that Evelyn Wood should have led that advance, and Chelmsford himself should have then led his men north over the Tugela drift. This is so theoretical that it is nonsense, ignoring the likely change in Cetshwayo's positioning of his *impis*. It has the smack of an amateur trying to sort out the logistics of a cranky machine. Forbes then applies his central criticism: that Chelmsford, 'instead of doing this, weak as he was, weakened himself yet further by chopping up his forces into four separate columns … I am not aware that he sent a request to Cetshwayo that he should be annihilated in detail, but indeed he almost might well have done so …'[40] Forbes was aware of the counter argument, explaining why Chelmsford did create the columns: he talks of the argument of 'friction' – this being the line of thought that sees huge problems in overcrowding in the transit of a massive force. But he responds with: 'The argument fails in the face of proven experience in South African marching … Pearson reached Eshowe from the Tugela in a few days …'[41]

In fact, what we have in the months following the disaster is a perfect case study in the nature of military intelligence at that time: the fundamental subject of accurate and relevant knowledge emerges into the light of debate. The colonials of various types all had knowledge that they expressed, and as we read, we realize that this kind of knowledge should have been in an intelligence dossier in Chelmsford's tent. For instance, on 3 February 'a colonial' wrote to *The Times* to offer some information: 'I suppose our Government is aware that the climate for some distance inland is most unhealthy –

in fact deadly – for the greater part of the year. The healthy season commences about May and ends in October.' The writer then adds information about the tsetse fly.[42]

In the response to Isandlwana, cavalry were to be dispatched, and this subject also raised questions that civilians or volunteers with information wanted to impart. It was a time when anyone could offer 'intelligence' because the high command at Whitehall, in their emphasis on the Great Game with Russia, had forgotten to compile gazetteers and cultural profiles for the officer class. For instance, Lovell Proctor, who had run a missionary station close to the battlefield, wrote concerning horses that were sent out being likely to suffer serious disease: 'I heard a very old trader observe that horses were only endangered by being allowed to eat the grass with the dew on it.'[43] Everything Chelmsford had done came under scrutiny. The letters pages of *The Times* were inundated with contributions from 'old soldiers' and 'settlers' and of course the usual tranche of amateurs and war theorists. Suddenly, almost everyone had an opinion on a topic related to military intelligence. Everything was contentious. Most of the discussion was on travel, transport and resources, and because there was a reliance on oxen for transport, this meant that only around eleven miles a day could be covered at the time of Chelmsford's move north, but even the basic fact of the time he chose to move was the subject of dissension. Many would have set off in May, to use the more dry and hard tracks. But the decision to have the columns move in January had the advantages of having pasture for the horses and oxen; also the Zulus would be short of food, and one of the key advantages was that the full rivers would help to provide the safety buffer that Natal needed in case of emergency.

It can be seen from this that Chelmsford's caution and adherence to set methods and lines of thought were not entirely wrongheaded. But a month after Isandlwana the debate raged. Some critics picked on British weapons and compared them unfavourably to the American weapons in the Civil War. Others always used India as the criterion of judgement, as in this from an anonymous writer: 'The

Zulus are better shots and better armed than the wild Asiatics with whom our troops in India have been dealing.'[44]

Many writers noted that a list of criticisms of weaponry, use of cavalry and intelligence planning must have been noted from shortcomings in the recent Kaffir Wars. Clearly, they had not been noted. The centre of discussion was on the wisdom of sending cavalry out to southern Africa. Julius Alington, who had hunted in the area for seventeen years, supported the use of cavalry: he listed several advantages, including the unsuitable nature of Natal horses (which seems a strange fact) – he argued that 'Natal horses are seldom more than 14 hands 3ins high, and though they are rarely lame and can do hard work on indifferent food, they have generally bad tempers and bad mouths and are as hard to lead as donkeys.' On the other hand, Lieutenant Colonel Robert Gunter, who had served with Durnford's column, pointed out that 'All the Native Contingent officers are mounted but the horses are suffering from a fever that was not known here two years ago, but is now very prevalent. My own horse is down with it and I must endeavour to get another tomorrow.'[45]

There is nothing like a free and open forum to bring out weaknesses, but in the context of the Zulu War this also shows how, because the army was still essentially 'fighting nature' more than the identified enemy, there was room for knowledge to be established and conformed, because a consensus was needed. A rifleman who had served in the Kaffir Wars argued that heavy regiments such as Dragoon Guards and the 17th lancers were the last troops to send to Natal. He pointed out that in 1847 and in 1851 those regiments had been out there and that the men were far too heavy for the Cape horses.

One of the most perceptive and constructive discussions was on the subject of balloons. There was also photography available at the time, of course, and combining these two makes complete sense in theory – a small captive balloon carrying a camera with sensitive plates could have soon located the positions of the Zulu *impis*. As Walter Woodbury pointed out, the work could have been done by 'The exposure being effected by means of electricity through the cord holding the balloon and ... by the latest strides made in the rapidity of dry plates, enabling views to be obtained even when swinging the camera in the hand.'[46]

On issues of transport, all kinds of suggestions were made, including plenty of argument for the use of mules. Every aspect of soldiering was open to scrutiny for the general public and ex-servicemen, amateurs and cranks all had plenty to say. Yet at the heart of all this was the undisputed fact that transport and communications had been integral to the fundamental criticisms, and this is very pointedly demonstrated in the case of Evelyn Wood in June 1878, when he led five companies and wagons from King Williams Town to Utrecht. It took five hours to get the wagons across the River Kei, a crossing of about eighty yards.

As for communications: although the Suez Canal had been opened in 1869 it still took sixty days for troops to get to the Cape. What this says is that the Cape had been seen as a distant, less important part of the Empire. From the beginning the Intelligence Division at the War Office had rationalized that towns in southern Africa existed simply to be garrisons for ships in transit elsewhere. Twenty-five years before Chelmsford's invasion, the Natal garrison had been explained by the lieutenant general at the time as being there only as a safety valve for civilians, in the event of an emergency. That is, the people could be shipped out and protected. The mindset for southern Africa was one of a transit fortress, as was the case with Gibraltar. For this reason, little attention had been given to communications until the Zulu emergency shone a light on the shortcomings. A letter from Chelmsford sent on 25 May did not reach the Duke of Cambridge (commander in chief of the armed forces) until 17 July.

The lessons of Isandlwana for military intelligence thinking were that traditional methods and strategies, previously used in Africa, did not work against every category of enemy, and that complicated organization and a lack of clear procedure and responsibility led to disaster. Just six years before the Zulu War, General Napier, President of the Council on Military Education, received a Prussian guest, a Major Roerdanz. He informed the assembled officers at the

United Services Institution about the finer points of the *kriegspiel* – the 'war game' – conceived by the War School at Cassel. The benefits of this, as was explained at the time, were that it gave 'excellent instruction in tactics and strategy', and second, that it taught officers 'to read maps with wonderful facility'.

The irony of this was surely not lost on those officers in Zululand and Natal who had attended or who had read about the new fad in the journals.

5

Khambula, Eshowe and Ulundi

After Isandlwana Chelmsford wrote home of course, but as the dispatch was taken by steamer via St Vincent it was 11 February before it reached London. What was about to happen, in the period between Isandlwana and Rorke's Drift, before the arrival of Lord Wolseley to take command in June, is what has been called The Middle War. That is a useful title, and it has its heroes. It was on the whole a productive interim campaign. At the end of January, Colonel Pearson remained to hold some of the southern area of Zululand, and he had dug in at Eshowe; Colonel Evelyn Wood moved to Khambula and set about a series of harassment actions. Of course, both Helpmakaar and Rorke's Drift were held too. As a writer in 1890 explained: 'The frontier of Natal was thus watched and guarded from end to end, and even if the Zulus, emboldened by their great success, had been tempted to make an inroad into the colony … they would have exposed themselves to attack at the flank and rear.'[47]

Evelyn Wood was one of the Wolseley 'Ring', the group of favoured officers around that charismatic leader, having fought with him in the Ashanti War. His career does not fit any pattern, as he began as a midshipman in the Navy and ended as Field Marshal. He had fought with distinction against the sepoys in the 1857 Indian Mutiny, and after staff posts and the Ashanti experience he was in the Eastern Cape Frontier War and then joined Chelmsford. He commanded the left flank of the Third Column. He commanded at

Khambula, and that action proved conclusively that, as at Rorke's Drift, the British strength was in fighting from entrenched, defensive positions where firepower would win the day. Despite the fact that the Zulu had taken Martini-Henry rifles at Isandlwana, they still lost when attacking a defensive laager.

Khambula is about fifteen miles from Utrecht to the west and Luneberg to the north; Wood had seen that the army forming the right horn of the usual form of attack, the inGobamakhosi, could be disrupted, largely because of the difficult terrain they had to cross. He realized that if he took them on with cavalry and drew them out, back to the laager, the firepower would cut them up. It took many hours to drive the Zulus back, and in the first stage they had taken a part of the defence area; not only were the rifles used, but the rockets also. Rockets were used in all the engagements between 22 January and 20 May. At Isandlwana they had not been used because of swamping by the sheer magnitude of the enemy forces and the swiftness of attack. But at Khambula, nine-pounder rockets were used and though they had only a minimal effect at least they were in action.

The Zulu centre came at Wood's men from a ridge then, and that was where the artillery came into their full effect: Wood wrote later that after the first two guns had done their work, the horses of the other four guns, under lieutenants Bigge and Slade, were sent inside the laager when the Zulus came within a hundred yards of them. Then, from the left arm of the Zulu force, the Uve and inGobamakhosi found themselves under heavy fire again, and their advance had to slow down due to the incline.

There was a determined chase of the fleeing warriors and Wood was later to be criticized for that, as there was a spirit of revenge in the British forces. Only the day before Wood had made a foolish mistake in the assault on Hlobane. That had been a huge mistake and over 200 British and natives had died. Wood and his staff had been in danger on that occasion, and his friend Captain Robert Campbell of the Coldstream Guards had been killed as Wood's party retreated. At Hlobane, the Frontier Light Horse had also been active, and they had led the early morning attack. Another friend of Wood's, Robert Barton, also died in that retreat. Therefore, there was an air of vengeance after the main confrontation at Khambula. The Zulu defeat was a very heavy one, and this victory surely turned the tide, doing something to repair the broken sense of honour after Isandlwana.

Zulu losses could have been around 2,000 and another 1,000 were injured. This kind of slaughter was what led Gladstone to say that thousands of Zulus died for no other offence than their attempt to defend against the artillery, and with their naked bodies, their hearths and home, their wives and families. When one of the principal Zulu leaders, Mbilini, was killed after a fight with Captain Prior's men in the Ntombe valley, the Zulu forces in the north of their territory faced a severe setback.

On the organizational side, there was a major piece of strategy going on at home. Chelmsford's appeal for huge reinforcements had caused a profound rethink about the high command in the very top reaches of the army. As six battalions were to be sent, the question arose about who would be the senior officers – the major generals. Strangely, it was Lady Frere who wrote to London specifically to ask that the head of the DQMG (Deputy Quartermaster General) for Intelligence at the War Office, Sir Archibald Alison, should be sent out. Alison was yet another of Wolseley's select men who had been in the Ashanti War with him. He had only one arm, but that did not stop him being a man of action. He had been important in the Cape Coast action and he led the Black Watch and Rait's Artillery against the Ashanti and had been in the thick of the action in the Crimea and in India. He was in charge of Intelligence until 1882 when he would again be in the field against Arabi in Egypt, with Wolseley.

The farce over choosing which four men would be the commanders in the reinforcements going to southern Africa is most informative about the attitudes to the Intelligence Branch, because Alison was not chosen. It is not difficult to find the reason why: the Duke of Cambridge was not exactly enthusiastic for Wolseley or any of his Ring. The men who were chosen were not at all rated well by Sir Garnet. On 13 February the commanders picked were Major General Henry Crealock, Edward Newdigate and Frederick Marshall, and Major General Henry Clifford was added later.

It is hard to overestimate the importance of this difference of opinion at the top level. Wolseley liked and approved of only one of the choices made by the Duke of Cambridge and his advisors: Clifford. Crealock had been with Wolseley in the Canadian campaign but had not impressed him, and in his opinion Frederick Marshall was an 'idiot'. What was happening in the years from circa 1870 to the present crisis in Natal was that there was a split: Cambridge favoured some officers and Wolseley favoured others. Men were assessed on their career record and of course also on their personalities.

This was an important factor in the establishment of the Intelligence Branch and also in the selection of the new men to join Chelmsford. But there is another layer of confusion to this, and that is in matters of seniority and responsibility. Who would replace whom if the necessity arose? Sir Henry Clifford (liked by all) was senior to Crealock, but the latter was defined as second-in-command to Chelmsford. The Duke of Cambridge insisted that Chelmsford had the power to give whatever commands he wanted to have one of them designated Chief of Staff. Thus, the same problem that had handicapped Chelmsford earlier in the advance into Zululand was there again: a lack of a full staff and clearly defined responsibilities. A triangle of dissension arose between Chelmsford, Crealock and Clifford. At the base of this were the achievements and aspirations of the Wolseley Ring. These 'new men' had absorbed the new creed from Sir Garnet, and although there were objections, the point was that actually in the field this new breed were excelling themselves.

Arguably a case in point in Zululand at the very time when the major generals were being appointed is that of Sir Evelyn Wood, and his work at Hlobane just before Khambula. This may have been almost a very large-scale disaster but it did at least show that field intelligence was improving in the southern African context. Wood was one of Wolseley's men and his use of field intelligence was almost always sound as he and Colonel Buller led the assault after information that the main Zulu army would be in Hlobane. He planned a pincer-movement attack and trusted in his intelligence source. Wood did not use infantry but designed a cavalry assault, arriving at dawn to surprise the enemy. Buller led 700 men towards the eastern side and Lieutenant Colonel Russell led the other wing with 250 men. Before moving, Buller had a camp set, with a fire, but this was a ruse, suggesting to Zulu scouts that they planned to wait for more men.

Hlobane is a plateau with a slope to one side, and Buller was sure there was a cattle track on that ascent, to use with his cavalry. He took his men steadily up and arrived before the Zulu were aware of them. That is a very significant fact: it means that for almost the first time, British troops had succeeded in doing what the Zulus had previously monopolized – attaining positions by stealth, using the terrain. Buller had his irregulars with him and as he reached the plateau, there were strings of cattle spread around and only small groups of warriors. In support, Russell had a problem: the western side could not be tackled by horsemen. He stayed down on the flat while apparently all was won on the plateau. But then the AbaQulusi *impis* were gathering at the north-east and they were moving to attack. Buller's men were encircled.

Sikhobobo, the *inDuna* (general) of the *impis*, knew that he could cut off Buller's men, having superior knowledge of the ground. But Wood was still ready to follow, and as far as field intelligence is concerned, Hlobane is an example of the triumph of accurate reports. Wood knew that Cetshwayo's main army was at Ulundi, and the King had sent his highly rated general, Mnyamana ka Ngqengelele, northwards with a huge army with instructions not to let courage overcome caution by attacking the British guns as at Rorke's Drift.

At Hlobane, a figure called Mthonga kaMpande, a rival of Cetshwayo, becomes important in the story of the intelligence in this conflict: he was with Wood as a scout, and he and his men were field spies. Their information on both Zulu thinking and on likely movements and emplacements was invaluable. But in the end, it was true grit as well as firepower that won the day. The Zulu army was close when Wood sent Russell to 'get into position on Zunguin Nek'. This was the western side of Hlobane (also called Zungen). Wood wanted him lower, at the foot of the plateau, but Russell moved to the slope, or saddle.

Communications and lack of maps again proved almost disastrous, because Buller found out very late that Captain Barton, mentioned earlier, should retreat speedily now that the position of the main Zulu force was known for sure. It was too late, and Barton and his men found themselves facing 10,000 Zulus. The British retreated, but the AbaQulusi were behind them and they were trapped. The British were chased and slaughtered. But Wood and Russell had seen this from on high and then went for the western end path, to open that up. A Victorian account of what happened next expresses it with the necessary drama:

> When the power level was at last reached there was still a long and weary march before the shattered band, and if the great Zulu army had attacked, the result must have been fatal. But, exhausted by their rapid movement from Ulundi, they did not close and Buller was able to bring off his men with very little further loss. That he did so was entirely due to his own undaunted courage and resolution.

He won his VC that day.

Colonel Pearson had been at Eshowe, close to the coast and only ten miles south of St Paul's, since 23 January. All he could do was hold the position and dig in, so he converted a mission station and he consolidated that, but the men there knew nothing of Isandlwana until 27 January. The place had been chosen as a depot with the future advance on Ulundi in mind – Cetshwayo's main kraal. The 1880 intelligence report described the situation as the place was fortified and Pearson merely waited for an expected attack: 'On three sides the fort was commanded at short range and some dangerous wooded ravine lay close below it. Plenty of good water was near at hand but there was no large stock of provisions at the fort.'[48] Further supplies were not really expected, and time wore on; by 6 February Pearson had a letter from Chelmsford advising him to retreat to the Lower Tugela, but Pearson replied that if supplies were sent by wagon, he could be well established. But by the 12 February no retreat was possible: Zulus were gathering around the fort. No attack came, but there was a notable advance in communications when a heliograph was used on 2 March, and then successfully the day after. The message decoded was extremely significant in the history of field intelligence: it was 'Look out for 1,000 men on the 13th, sally out when you see me to …' It was not fully understood, but on 5 March this was decoded: 'From Colonel Law to Colonel Pearson. About 13th instant … I advance to your support with 1,000 men … Be prepared to sally out to meet me …'[49]

Chelmsford had made it clear that he was going to relieve Eshowe as soon as he had the new reinforcements from home. He was delighted with the success of the heliograph (although at first this was merely a substitute, as discussed in chapter 8). He noted in a letter to the Secretary of State that 'I am happy to say that last night I received information that communication from and to Eshowe, by means of flashing lights, was established.' It was a small step forward, but in intelligence terms it was a stunning achievement.

The reinforcements began to arrive; after that in terms of military intelligence and the use of spies, there was arguably the most significant event in the war when John Dunn, who had lived with the Zulus and who had been on friendly terms with Cetshwayo, crossed to the British side. He was settled with his family, as noted in chapter 3, near the Thukela river. Of course, through Zulu eyes he would have been the worst kind of traitor. Here was a man who knew the Zulu culture and language intimately; he would know in detail how the people thought in terms of military strategy, and he was familiar with beliefs, rituals and taboos. But the most significant boon for Chelmsford was that he had a network of spies. These were, in Zulu, *izinDuna* – and Magumbi, whose activities have not yet been widely described, gave a full report on the Zulu force at Eshowe. He gave precise figures for manpower and location, and most important of all, he said that there was a state of confusion in the land because Cetshwayo gave so many orders and these were puzzling and illogical or unclear. It was natural that Chelmsford, now knowing that the Zulu forces were scattered and that there was a hint of desperation in the report that even the sick warriors were being called back, needed to act fast: he planned the advance of his columns, but this time with an eye to defence and to adaptation. He could not accept without question Magumbi's report, of course; caution was essential. He had a total force of almost 6,000 British and auxiliaries and every command he gave was saturated with the awareness of previous failure. Shock and despair had changed him, and he had come through. For all the criticisms against the man, it cannot be denied that he had his tactical faculties under full command this time. He was definite about the need for laagering the wagons and was precise on the need to have ammunition ready and accessible. He even used the border agents and pockets of troops entrenched there, directing them to create diversions so that the Zulu force might be weakened. After all, although the main report was that there were about 15,000 ready to fight in the Eshowe area, there had also been other sources which suggested that there could be twice that number. Unfortunately there was no heliograph on every peak and plateau.

Lying uneasily beneath some of the orders there is a tone and attitude suggesting more than a little nervousness and a little of the headmaster instructing the first eleven: 'These parties will remain quietly on the alert. No smoking, no talking above a whisper and only regarding matters of duty. Their duty is to listen ...'[50] The new column was on its way in late March and from this point on there is a definite prominence in the activities of all elements of field intelligence – on both sides. It is clear from contemporary accounts that Zulu scouts were always in evidence.

It is obvious, now that the area of activity was more closely circumscribed, that Chelmsford could more easily be aware of the enemy. For instance, he noted in one report that border agents had seen a large Zulu force moving eastwards from the north-west of his position. He countered by moving for specified distances and then laagering. When camp was made close to Gingindlovu they were only eighteen miles from Eshowe, and what happened then was something that would not have been possible in January: John Dunn and Captain Molyneux went into spying mode, venturing close to the Zulus in the misty night. Dunn acted like a character from a *Boys' Own* story book, swimming over the river to move close enough to see the bivouacked warriors. Suspicions were confirmed: a large force was there and they would attack at dawn, in all probability.

This was at the Nyezane, and Chelmsford was up against some leaders from the January campaigns, including Prince Dabulamanzi whose home was close to Eshowe. Dunn's earlier spy reports had been accurate and reflect how he had been to see personally what the situation was. The British were in a strong position; troops were ready to move into position at half past six when the Zulu advance was seen and monitored. The enemy moved to the left front, crossing the Nyezane, and then they assumed their usual formation of head and horns, the right 'horn' coming from the Misi hill. But after Rorke's Drift, British confidence was well on the rise when it came to being surrounded when dug in and with knowledge of the enemy numbers.

Captain Hart, another Ashanti War veteran, had had a narrow escape from a previous encounter with the Zulus at the Wombane Hill, and now he was there in the laager. He wrote an account later, stating that he saw 'the most splendid piece of skirmishing the eye ever beheld', and he watched the warriors, profoundly impressed, adding, 'If total concealment were possible, we should not have seen a Zulu till he reached our trench.'[51] The attack was determined and brave, and it has to be noted that the Gatling gun was in action here, a confrontation blandly noted by Chelmsford at the time, but with the passage of history this adds significantly to the Zulu reputation for extreme courage. Warriors ran and circled, taking cover where they could to find a shooting position, but their volleys did little harm compared to the incessant fire from the British. Men were cut down in hundreds.

Chelmsford then ordered the cavalry out, later with the native contingent in support. There was then a charge with swords swinging, the mounted infantry then gathering to follow suit. Again, as was the case at Khambula, the pursuit of the fleeing warriors was relentless; Hart summed it up when he wrote, 'Chivalry ends when pursuit begins.' Chelmsford reported that the Zulus had a thousand dead on that field. The British casualties of dead and wounded came to just sixty-one.

Chelmsford and Pearson then met outside Eshowe and the relief of that garrison came. Although Chelmsford had decided to abandon the fort at Eshowe, much to Pearson's disappointment, his revised plan highlights something important for military intelligence, as indeed does his decision to destroy the home of Dabulamanzi. This is concerned with the important element within the area of 'knowledge of the enemy' which includes all the imagery, ritual and menace in war normally called 'respect'. Chelmsford, in the confident flush of two victories and having had his enemy on the run twice, still fully acknowledged the public image of fear and respect that the Zulu nation created.

He destroyed Dabulamanzi's kraal as a 'PR gesture' much as a fighter marks territory and achieves something that is more a signal for attention than a definite achievement of any note. As he had now come to understand, 'knowing' the Zulu meant being aware of the impact of their whole battle psyche. Not only had Shaka, when he established the Zulu military state a generation earlier, made a military structure: he had also formed a mindset of assumed victory. He understood that stage one of a victory is in the first fearful impression – the lighting of a fire of panic and terror in the opposition. Officers and men who wrote reports and memoirs of these campaigns all were struck by the sound, colour and panache of the Zulu *impis*. The sounds of assegais on shields as they moved, the songs and chants, the deep impression of a body of men moving and thinking with one mind: these made the 'respect' something related to a kind of knowledge of the enemy that only those men such as Dunn could really perceive.

Chelmsford was going back to the Thukela, but only to prepare for the last push to what he saw as the ultimate triumph over Cetshwayo: to defeat him at his own kraal and take him prisoner. That meant a campaign on Ulundi. Ulundi, known to the Zulu as oNdini, was the royal kraal of the King, constructed after Cetshwayo ascended the crown in 1873, on a plain bordered by hills, on well-drained soil. The arrangement was that there was a parade ground area in the centre and huts were around that, with a predominance of older, married men (who had distinctive white shields) based there. The huts had floors of clay and then the fire in the centre would bellow smoke that would find its way through the thatching. Special areas in the compound were for the King's wives and family, and these quarters were called the *isigodlo*. There were more than 1,000 huts and usually there were over 2,000 people living there. Because it was also a barracks for the inGobamakhosi regiment, the King's favourite, it would always be well defended. The regiment or corporation of warriors was called an *amabutho*, and that concept was important for the British intelligence personnel to grasp, as it related to what was previously said about ritual and confidence. It was a bonded corps, with specific allegiance.

Naturally, the British forces made this the objective. However, there were several kraals that the King used, and that was to be a problem when it came to tracking him down after the battle at Ulundi. There had been various royal kraals made since the 1850s and so clearly the reports, from Dunn, about this particular one were to help Chelmsford in determining his route after the reinforcements had arrived and he had conceived his strategy. Cetshwayo referred to the place as his favourite – in Zulu, his *komkhulu*. The kraal was the very heart of thc *amabutho* system.

What was on Chelmsford's side now was that, after long campaigns and considerable losses in warrior numbers, the Zulus were not at their best; the British now could muster over 10,000 regular troops, and although the Zulus had approximately 25,000 fighters, they were not exactly brimming with confidence after the failure at Eshowe. But there was an obstacle to progress, and as usual with Natal, it was concerned with status and responsibility. Sir Henry Bulwer objected to the native contingents being sent to do border patrols and would not let them come under the sway of Chelmsford in his grand new plan. Chelmsford complained in letters home to the very top – the Duke of Cambridge – but nevertheless, he had to carry on and work without the auxiliaries.

Chelmsford in his fresh mindset was a different man, and his thought and orders display someone who had learned to use the intelligence he now had coming reliably, and to use it with an eye to the overall strategy. The first step in this was to keep the warriors away from food. His idea, probably coming from Dunn, was that incursions by small patrols from the border, which was now held firmly by British troops, would keep the Zulus active and preoccupied, and so not able to gather food, as this was the time of year when that would normally happen. Again, the border agents came into prominence. Fannin was once more a very useful information source, and this time he was actually involved in some of the sorties into Zululand. What happened was that because there were large numbers of auxiliaries available to cross the river into enemy territory, the Zulus had to respond; they did so by staging retaliations against settlers or anyone else who was in their way. It was still certain, however, that the Zulu *impis* were by no means ready to give in. On the contrary, they knew that it was only a matter of time before the British came at them in considerable numbers. Their intelligence was always wide, adaptable and able to penetrate into any areas of this theatre of war.

Chelmsford had the upper hand in terms of morale, and everyone was aware that since the miserable defeats and errors of January and February, there was a feeling that the tide was up, the ascendancy was there to be won. The question was what strategy was best? The columns were sorted, and new commanders allotted their roles. Crealock was in charge of the First Column – Pearson's men from Eshowe and others; Evelyn Wood was retained with his men, and they were called the Flying Column; then Newdigate was given command of the final group. Chelmsford kept the First Column closer to the coast and their task was to attack and destroy a particular kraal. They were to be in the territory that Dunn knew very well. The largest column with Newdigate would aim at Ulundi directly and of course Crealock's would move west, crossing the Thukela.

The Flying Column would move from Khambula. It was then merely a question of deciding the exact route towards Ulundi. On the Zulu side, Cetshwayo was well aware that his army was able to have one last large-scale offensive and he was well informed about his likely predicament should the columns all perform as directed. Cetshwayo was caught between negotiation and action. He sent messengers in an attempt to set up some talks and of course to play for time. His armies needed reorganization and of course there were the younger men coming through to fight, so he had to put time on his side rather than continue with the usual tactics against a now much stronger and wiser enemy. As in the original meeting at which impossible terms were set for Cetshwayo, so Chelmsford used the same ploy again, stating that he would have to have all firearms handed in and a very large number of cattle given as reparations payment.

This was all diplomacy and naturally Chelmsford gained, particularly as Crealock's column near the coast was moving so slowly. Dunn spoke with Sintwangu, a special messenger, and it was clear from this that Dunn knew there was no question of peace. With hindsight, it is remarkable what a difference there was in that situation compared to the January advance, when there was no one in the ranks of the columns with Dunn's knowledge and status.

All forces progressed and by 29 June, on Entonjaneni Hill, just sixteen miles from Ulundi, it was decided that the troops would then advance, moving lightly with supplies behind. Wolseley, approaching Fort Pearson, was now to be consulted as he was to come and take control, and Chelmsford wrote to him of the movements he was undertaking. The Zulus had not crossed the river to confront them, so there was time to gather maximum levels of manpower. Once again, Buller did excellent work, taking his men across to scout, and he discovered not only the positions but also the numbers of the enemy across the river. The intelligence report of 1880 notes the importance of this: 'By this reconnaissance information was gained as to the nature of the country between Umvolosi and Ulundi, and as to the strength and position of the enemy forces.'[52] The Umfolozi (as spelled today) in question was the White Umfolozi, running south of Ulundi. The Black Umfolozi was parallel, much further to the north.

The advance to Ulundi then began, and the army was in a rectangular formation, the troops on the sides being in ranks of four; they had passed a kraal called the Nodwengu (another former royal kraal) when the Zulus came from all directions. The Gatlings and artillery did severe damage and the Zulu accuracy in rifle fire was very poor. The depth of the infantry ranks withstood the various switches in direction of the Zulu forces, and gradually the attack weakened, enabling Chelmsford to call the 17th Lancers into action. These pursued the Zulus towards the hills. The 1880 report notes that 'in this pursuit the efficacy of the lance as a cavalry weapon was abundantly proved'.[53]

There was also Buller and his cavalry and they followed up. Then Ulundi itself was shelled. Cetshwayo left the kraal and his army accepted defeat. On 5 July, Wolseley received the good news at Fort Pearson. Chelmsford's work in Zululand was over and he resigned his command. Yet again, many blamed him for a retreat because after entering Ulundi and going into the royal kraal (which was full of bottles of champagne and gin) he saw that there was no Zulu attempt to rally and he withdrew. He did not set about chasing and locating the fleeing Cetshwayo either. That was to be left to Wolseley, who had written to John Maurice from Cyprus in February that he was 'lost in astonishment at the folly of the Government allowing the command to fall into Crealock's hands and I have now made up my mind that nothing short of a miracle can possibly save the Government. They will be wrecked on the Zulu rock … who is at the bottom of this business I know not.'[54]

One of the most informative sources for a deeper understanding of Chelmsford is the material regarding his defence of himself and his actions in the face of Archibald Forbes' criticisms (discussed in chapter 8). On 14 July he wrote to Wolseley: 'With regard to my plan of campaign is it of course, like any other, fair grounds for criticism – I am anxious, however, to let you know that had I to begin operations again I should make no change whatsoever in my operations with the distributions of my troops.'[55] Writers such as Forbes were beginning to play a part in intelligence thinking, and had done so since the Crimean War. Chelmsford was rattled by the attack and it forced him to explain his strategy as he had not done before. The central onslaught from Forbes had been about 'intercommunication and mutual support' and Chelmsford responded with: 'In a country like Zululand, as in Afghanistan, there is no possibility of intercommunication and mutual support – each column as I have already said was supposed to be strong enough to fight alone, and I have never heard any doubt that either Colonel Pearson or Colonel Wood felt any doubt in their own minds on this point …'[56]

Chelmsford was heartily sick of southern Africa and made that very plain to Wolseley, who had been appointed Commander in Chief and High Commissioner for Natal and the Transvaal. When Wolseley did call on Chelmsford, hoping to talk with him, he missed him and wrote a note saying that he wished to build 'a golden bridge' for Chelmsford to retire by.

Disraeli back home, already hugely disenchanted with Chelmsford, told Queen Victoria that his move back out of Ulundi was his last and crowning mistake. The Duke of Cambridge responded sharply too, saying, 'The distinguished generals fear that if there is any fight left in the Zulus this hurried withdrawal of troops and staff must tell very greatly against in its moral effect against us.'[57]

6

The Hunt for Cetshwayo

In his biography of Sir Garnet Wolseley, John Maurice wrote that the capture of Cetshwayo was 'a necessary preliminary to any permanent pacification of the country'. It was not an easy task, and Maurice was the intelligence officer entrusted with the chase. At first, the area of land within which the King could safely be assumed to be inside was cordoned with troops, and then, when intelligence was received, Maurice set off with a party of the 19th Hussars and Major Barrow and Lord Gifford, who was the leader of the native scouts. What followed was an object lesson in the use and reliability of information given to intelligence staff.

Edric Frederick Gifford was born in 1849, the son of the 2nd Baron Gifford. After Harrow he joined the 83rd Foot in 1869. He became Lord Gifford in 1872 and two years later he was a lieutenant in the 2nd Battalion, 24th Foot – later the South Wales Borderers. He was yet another officer who was with Wolseley in the Ashanti War, and he won the VC in that conflict. He was in charge of the scouts and was truly remarkable and heroic, seeking out the enemy and gauging their plans. He sought out enemy positions and took prisoners. His VC citation states that he dogged the enemy movements and captured many enemies single-handed. Before the taking of Becquah in 1874 he entered the city and took note of enemy positions. In 1879 he was with Wolseley as aide-de-camp and, as his specialty was field reconnaissance and he was accustomed to working with native scouts, he was ideal for the task of working with Maurice in the search for Cetshwayo.

The other officer involved, Major Percy Barrow, began his army career as a cornet in the 19th Hussars in 1868. He served at The Curragh two years before coming to southern Africa as a special service officer: again, scouting was his forte, as he worked with Pearson's column scouting the border, and he was present at Nyezane. Despite being quite seriously wounded in the leg, he had recovered sufficiently to join Maurice and Gifford. Major Ashe of the Dragoon Guards later wrote a memoir, and in that he pays tribute to Barrow in an earlier encounter, saying that Barrow's men were so adept at scouting around the immediate country that the Zulu spies 'who swarmed around' could not find any way to get close enough to learn the real strength of Ashe's column.

During the hunt for Cetshwayo, Maurice kept Wolseley informed of progress. On 17 August he wrote that he was in the King's kraal with Gifford, a linguist and two Basutos. He wrote that he thought there was 'a pretty strong scent' and he had been given information that Cetshwayo was trying to get through the east to the Jukhanda people and he believed that he would pass near to Ulundi the next day. But in fact he had gone north, as was realized later, and stayed with Chief Zibhebhu, and then moved – on his own – to a position north of the Black Umfolozi river.

On 18 August, Maurice was at another kraal and seven miles ahead of Barrow when he captured a man and girl carrying a lanyard that belonged to Cetshwayo. But Maurice was trusting very little, and when the man said he had been sent by a certain Usibelo, Maurice instilled some fear into him by threatening to burn down the kraal where they were. This was the beginning of a wild goose chase, as Maurice took the man with him, after the prisoner had sworn that he wanted to see the King captured. The man asked for a hundred head of cattle if he took the British to where the King was. Maurice reported that 'He promises to tell us everything.'[58]

Also reported on 18 August was Maurice's meeting with various parties of Zulus who had details of the King. He found a group of women who had been personal attendants of Cetshwayo and on them he found a lot of property that had belonged to the fugitive. This included a Martini-Henry and a fowling piece. Maurice was sure that he had enough information to find the man, and told Wolseley that the King had an injured leg, and that he had at least two men with him, but had lost all his horses. He reported that he knew the King's whereabouts the day before and Gifford was totally confident of success, saying that they were closing in, and that Wolseley, coming north, would meet them within a week.

Then matters went into an uneasy stage: Gifford became worried about Barrow being too far off and without any definite orders; Maurice claimed to have thought this through, however, writing that there was only one way that Cetshwayo could have gone and that he would run into Barrow before long. But there was rumour and misinformation in transit all the time. After one note to Wolseley, Maurice wrote: 'P.S. I wrote the above under the impression that Barrow had caught the King.'[59]

By 22 August, Maurice wrote that Gifford was sure they would 'nab their man' quickly, but it was at that point that Maurice became aware that his source had been 'lying unmercifully'. The man who had been their hostage as they travelled swore that he would take them to the very spot where the King had been seen, and one of the most farcical events in the intelligence actions of the war followed. Maurice said, 'We therefore threatened to shoot him if he led us wrong and he pointed out a piece of dense bush under a cliff in a certain valley about seven miles from us.'[60]

Gifford and Maurice went to the spot and Gifford deployed scouts at important points en route. Then the Maurice party dismounted, left their horses with Basuto auxiliaries and began to beat the bush under a crest of a cliff. Maurice drew a sketch of this later, and he recalled that as they moved they heard gunshots. Running to the sound of the guns, they found no Cetshwayo – simply an escape attempt by the man they had trusted. The two leaders then had a rethink and Maurice wrote that they had decided to sit and 'work this out'. Progress was made, however, when Gifford reported that he had actually found a place that had been prepared especially for the King. It was one of the sacred places, one he apparently visited as he moved around. The information on him was that he never travelled far, going to neighbouring kraals which were his supply depots.

Maurice concluded that he had too few mounted men to succeed in the chase, saying, 'There is an amount of ground to be beaten down to actually get him, which is too much for our own weak number of mounted men.'[61]

Yet, as all this was in progress, as Lieutenant Amyatt-Burney recorded, another patrol was about to be lucky. A note was passed to Major Marter saying 'Have got on the track again. Hope to take him tonight.' As the party with Marter moved forward towards a stream a Zulu approached and gave them a tip as to which direction to take, saying 'I have had my say.' In a kraal by the Ngome Forest, after the patrol had advanced stealthily, there were twenty-three people, and some shots were fired, but the kraal was surrounded and Marter was led to the hut where Cetshwayo was. The King asked, 'What rank does the officer hold to whom I am to surrender?' Cetshwayo trusted the interpreter and came out of his hut. He was taken into exile, at Port Durnford for the first stage, then on to Cape Town where he was kept in the old castle. In 1883 he was back in Zululand and was allowed to make a new kraal, supervised constantly of course.[62]

As an interim adventure, the search had served several useful purposes for the intelligence officers: the seasoned Zulu campaigners were mixing with the new arrivals, and notes were compared, with the Zulu discussed alongside the Ashanti and of course various enemy tribes in India and Afghanistan. What they could all find agreement on was the improved communication methods, ranging from scouting parties to border guards and from interpreters to methods of messaging.

Wolseley split Zululand into regions and Dunn had his land apportioned, back in his former area beyond the Thukela. Boundary work was soon initiated, land was given to chiefs who had sided with Britain, and border rulers were allotted 'residents' on the East India Company pattern. The avuncular guidance of British imperialism was soon put in place. But Wolseley was not confident he could achieve the settlement well. As Maurice, writing the biography of his commander later in life, noted, 'He seemed out of sympathy with his subject and out of touch with his surroundings.'[63]

7

Personnel and Personalities

At this stage in the narrative of events and the part played by field intelligence in the war, it is useful to summarize the people who were influential in the intelligence initiatives at the time, both in theoretical terms and in the very practical arm of intelligence work, scouting and communications in the terrain of warfare. The following are arguably the most prominent individuals in the war with regard to affairs of diplomacy, knowledge of the enemy and field intelligence in the war.

GARNET WOLSELEY AND JOHN FREDERICK MAURICE

In 1903 a special publication, *The Report of His Majesty's Commissioners on the War in southern Africa*, criticized the organization and management of the Anglo-Boer War. Every contributing department of the military machine of the Empire was called to question, with the exception of the Intelligence Branch and its leader. As the historian Correlli Barnet has noted, as early as 1896 the Department of Military Intelligence had informed the general staff that it would take two months for reinforcements to reach troops in southern Africa, and that at that time there should have been an increase in manpower in that region. That detail might not sound like such a momentous fact, but it was, and the reason for that was that even after twenty-three years the Intelligence brains were not necessarily awarded any status or seen as particularly noteworthy by many in positions of power.

Yet over that twenty-three years there had been a quiet revolution. Before the founding of the Intelligence Branch in 1873, the so-called 'Long Peace' between 1815 and the Crimean War had been largely a matter of complacency and neglect in terms of the growth of intelligence as a respected department of a war ministry and military structure. The Great Game, in one sense, was peripheral, rather amateur and always somehow overshadowed by the machinations of diplomacy. It is not difficult to see the activities of the spies and surveyors out in the Raj and the Levant as secondary to the larger questions of maintaining the power base nearer home.

Of course, the Crimea and the Mutiny changed all that. Despite the poor reputation that posterity has given to Lord Raglan, at least he saw the importance of military intelligence. As John Hughes-Wilson has written,

> The fact was, in the long peace, the British Army had forgotten how to collect intelligence. The Great Duke's legacy has much to answer for. Lord Raglan … railed at his lack of intelligence. The truth is that Raglan was a calculating and sophisticated commander.'[64]

By 1870, that type of commander was exactly what was needed. The Franco-Prussian War had taught the rest of Europe a lesson about how to conduct warfare: the Prussians had beaten France because of their short-term service system and their reservist corps. They had seen the value of streamlining provisions, from uniform victualling to transport, and they had highlighted the value of having truly professional soldiers. In Britain in 1870 the army still worked by the system of purchase of commissions. The Empire was ticking over with surprising ease when one considers that most British officers bought their commissions, as they had been doing for as long as there was an Empire. But at the time when the Intelligence Branch was set up, the new theorists and army professionals were beginning to be a presence, and much of this change was down to the Gladstone ministry and in particular Edward Cardwell, who became Secretary of State for War in 1868. In addition to ending the flogging that was common practice in the army, he had Gladstone's help in abolishing the purchase system. When the Lords blocked his Army Regulation

Bill in 1874, Gladstone went to the Queen and used her power to see the legislation through. Victoria did this because she could not tolerate the terrible row this subject had caused in her government factions.

Cardwell has been called the armourer of Britain. In his Army Enlistment Act of 1870 he introduced short service and in many ways this was to open up possibilities of radical change in the perception of the place and importance of military intelligence. Prussia had benefited from a large reserve of experienced men who had done a limited term service and yet were standing by for action when required. Cardwell brought in a six-year term and opened up a more rigid selection procedure. The army had long been defined as the depository of criminals and renegades, the tough types who had won the field at Waterloo, perhaps, but in late Victorian years it was perceived that there was more to being an officer than dash and horsemanship, and there was more to being a squaddie than drill and hard drinking.

It was in these momentous years, circa 1870 to 1874, that the Intelligence Branch arrived, and a man whose attitudes to the army matched the new thinking came along at the right time, following Sir Richard Brackenbury in 1887: Sir Garnet Wolseley. One of the men who was to be a principal figure in many departments of army functions was the future Brigadier William Robertson, a man from a modest background in rural Lincolnshire. In his memoirs he writes of the birth of this branch:

> When first formed in 1873 it was a branch of the Quartermaster-General's Department; later it was placed under the Adjutant-General; and was, when I joined it, more or less under the Commander in Chief, Lord Wolseley. It had a staff of about sixteen officers and, with the 'Mobilisation Section' of three or four officers, was the only semblance of a General Staff then in existence. The Mobilisation Section had originally been under the Director of Military Intelligence, was afterwards absorbed by the Adjutant-General's department and then, like the Intelligence Branch, came under the Commander in Chief.[65]

Robertson added that the two branches had been 'constantly tossed over from one high official to another'. He noted that intelligence organization was therefore always going to be influenced by whoever was in charge at one particular time. Clearly, there was a problem in how the department and its work were seen by the top brass. What Stieber had achieved in Prussia was certainly interesting in its outcomes, but the thinking was that there was no way that Britain was going to ape the Prussians in Stieber's own brand of espionage. The bottom line was that the most useful intelligence work that had been done since the war with Napoleon had been done by individuals – by people like Cattley or Abbot – and so it took some time for the new department to have a clear identity. Robertson explains the early work done there, in the office at 29 Queen Anne's Gate, as primarily the collection and collation of information on foreign countries. He also notes that such knowledge was somehow to be processed, taken into the catalogue of current information on every state that might play a part in conflict, and kept for reference.

Before this new departure, according to Sir George Aston, the prevailing attitudes had been more domestic:

> The military authorities were still under the influence of the Palmerston Royal Commission of the early sixties, which was responsible for the idea that fortifications could do the work of warships, the theory being that the introduction of steam propulsion had rendered obsolete Raleigh's old principle that it was better to deal with foreign invading armies at sea … intelligence in those early years was mainly devoted to studying how to deal with a foreign invading army …[66]

In the 'long peace' the army had been more interested in tactics than in strategy, but that was going to change. The initiative began with a memo from Stanhope (who was later to be chairman of the Central Committee) in June 1888. This defined the aims of the new branch in three main functions: the support of the civil power, the provision of staff for the India garrison and the capability of mobilizing corps of regular and auxiliary troops. What was happening behind all this was the emergence of forward-planning with regard to geopolitics: the event of a war with a European power or wars in the Raj. The subtext, we might guess, was again something gleaned from Prussian professionalism: to have an intelligence arm of the forces that would have an important status and that would be part of an organic function in time of war.

In 1875 came the Hartington Commission, which recommended a war office department with a chief of staff whose business would be largely that of collecting information. In fact, in the person of Wolseley this kind of function had begun, as he set about creating a fresh breed of officer and placed intelligence within a generally more forward-looking and educated elite of senior staff. However, although the new branch was initially under Sir John Ardagh's command, at the time of its formation Wolseley was in West Africa, leading the expeditionary force against the Ashanti, and this provides an enlightening case study in which we may see the new attitudes at work, particularly as Wolseley was destined to take over the branch later. Wolseley, in the words of one of his biographers, saw that 'War was a serious business and soldiering a profession, not a pastime for dilettantes. The days of playing at soldiers were over. Education in the army, still at a dangerously low ebb, should permeate through all ranks.'[67]

Cardwell and Wolseley were an alliance, and they were not alone. Other officers had been nurtured into supporting roles. Cardwell, when the Ashanti problem became a most urgent one, made sure that Wolseley would lead the force out there and we have to reflect that both were out to prove something about the new methods and attitudes. The Ashanti King, Kofi, and other warlords were conducting a brutal and inhuman regime of terror along the coast and into the territory of the Fanti. Their militaristic structures combined with bloodthirsty acts of murder and repression led to a state of emergency in which the various British administrators of smaller protectorates feared that a very large-scale emergency might arise if something were not done.

Garnet Wolseley was born in 1833 and became perhaps a name on every Victorian's lips when Gilbert and Sullivan made him the 'very model of a modern major-general' referred to in the 'Major-General's Song' in *The Pirates of Penzance.* He rose to brevet lieutenant colonel in just eight years and he was always in the thick of the action, losing an eye in the Crimea and suffering a severe wound in Burma. He became known in military circles as much for his book, *The Soldier's Pocket Book*, published in 1869, as for his campaigns. As mentioned previously, his Ring was to be massively influential in all kinds of contexts in Victorian warfare.

Wolseley put the emphasis on gathering the right team of officers around him and then planned to use native fighters, with a request to the high command that regular troops would be ready to arrive if needed. He even gave his superiors a quote for the job of £150,000. Wolseley also involved the Navy, for diplomatic reasons, and so the force that eventually arrived and set about marching on Kumasi, the Ashanti main settlement, was a mixed one in which some of the fiercest African warriors were travelling along with a naval detachment and Fanti people. But Wolseley realized at a later stage of planning that he would need some professional soldiers from Britain and he had no less a force than the Black Watch with him. One of those officers recalls him 'bright-eyed, confident and smiling' while sitting in a Madeira cane chair, which was carried by some burly Fantees, 'his staff around him'. His charisma was there from the start.

Wolseley had officers whose task it was to survey local conditions and also to collect a viable force of local fighters. Indicative of the new thinking was the nature of the key men in the Wolseley team. There was Lieutenant Maurice who was an instructor from Sandhurst, Captain Buller, Major Colley, and the future principal of the Intelligence Branch, the colourful Captain Brackenbury. But perhaps the most significant feature of the early phase of the Ashanti campaign was Garnet Wolseley's own habits: he studied blue books and reports assiduously and he worked his way through all the information about the place and people that he could find. As Joseph Lehmann noted:

> For the first time in the history of the British Empire, a general appointed to command an expedition sat down to a table at the War Office with the Secretary for War, the Secretary for the

> Colonies, the First Lord of the Admiralty and the various heads of military departments to discuss the necessary arrangements.[68]

There was a library of books on topography and history available for the staff to peruse. Not to put too fine a point on it, this was *intelligent* intelligence in war.

One of the heroes of the Ashanti campaign, Sir Henry Brackenbury, took over the Army Intelligence command in the 1880s and according to Sir George Aston a significant change occurred … it began to be realized that gathering information about foreign armies was only a means to an end. The next step must be to make the best possible use of whatever army Parliament consented to provide, and at last the question of speedy mobilization, which Prussia had taught to the world in 1870, was grasped. This implies that Robertson's narrative does not make it clear that it took a good ten years for the lessons from Prussia to be learned. In fact, when Robertson talks about his training course at the staff college, the importance of the Franco-Prussian War for the changes in British intelligence becomes clearer. Robertson was taught at the college by Colonel George Henderson, whom he refers to warmly as 'Hender' – the man who was to be Director of Intelligence with Lord Roberts in the Boer War.

Robertson and his fellow students were taken to see the battlefields of the Franco-Prussian War, notably to Wœrth and Spicheren where the French had been defeated and the action was followed by very demanding armistice terms by Bismarck. Robertson's account of the Staff College education provides a clear example of the new attitudes in practice. He spends a lot of time in his autobiography recalling his efforts to learn foreign languages and to master administration, yet intellectual discourse on tactics and on the application and use of intelligence is always balanced with this theory. He gives a clear impression of the kind of mindset expected of the young officers attached to intelligence work, based on a conversation he had with Henderson:

> Having passed into the college without the help of a crammer I was anxious as to how my work there would compare with

> that of the other officers, and so I told the commandant at the first interview … His encouraging reply was that the lack of this form of education need not necessarily be a handicap. 'We do not want crammers here – we want officers to absorb, not to cram.'[69]

The Franco-Prussian War had put tactics, theoretical intelligence and mobilization at the forefront of military studies. Arguably, it was that conflict that most brought about the revisionary thinking about the need for an Intelligence Branch. Wolseley was one of the leaders in that generation influenced by the new approaches to warfare. Basically, the Prussian victory had been so swift and complete that it furnished a template of success.

But the new department still needed to be placed somewhere in the structure of the army. By the time of the office of Sir Henry Campbell-Bannerman in 1892, the Intelligence Department was put, as so often in the past, under the Adjutant General. Since the 1880s the department had been streamlined in many ways, and there is ample evidence to show that its briefs, assignments and staff were busy doing what intelligence outfits have always done when there is too much to cope with: prepare voluminous reports. For instance, in 1882 John Frederick Maurice, secretary to Wolseley with the Ashanti, wrote a *History of the Campaigns of 1882 in Egypt*. This was prepared specifically for the branch. Best Jervis's lessons on cartography had been absorbed by this time, as the volume has eleven maps on no fewer than sixteen folding sheets. Maurice even appends a map illustrating the attack on Tel el-Kebir.

We have to ask, though, about the other side of intelligence, the one involving people rather than paper. What was happening out in the field of operations at this same time? A rare insight is provided by Wolseley himself, writing in his campaign journal while in the relief expedition to Khartoum in 1884. Just before Christmas, when he perhaps had a little more leisure to fill a few pages, he wrote:

> It is always difficult to get information in a country where money is no temptation to its people to betray it, and the cruelties of barbarous people not only to the spy but to all his family make men hesitate before they undertake to give the

> invader information. In Europe or America of course money will provide the energetic man with any amount of information …[70]

He and his fellow officers were learning in these years that understanding the cultural and ethnic lifestyles and relationships in the localities of warfare was more complex than previously thought. In fact, the Raj in India had become a touchstone, a model of how to do things in this respect. But as with all templates of the kind, the situation there does not necessarily carry across to other contexts. There was no 'John Company' in Africa and comparisons with European races and traditions, as Wolseley was realizing, had no value in places such as the Sudan. In that same journal he assesses the place of the Mahdi, the leader of the Sudanese rebellion, in this respect:

> Of course native rumours are important and generally contain some grains of truth in them but they are apt to frighten those whose nerves are not the strongest. One day I hear the Mahdi is surrounded by thousands of warriors longing to die for him … the rumours and stories I hear seriously repeated by fairly sensible men very often here are to me simply ludicrous …[71]

Under two men, Major General Sir Patrick MacDougall (who had been in charge of the Camberley Staff College) and Captain Wilson, the new branch really went into full throttle by the time of Wolseley's relief assignment in Egypt. That expeditionary army took with it several copies of a massive 400-page volume called the *Handbook on Eqypt*, which had in its covers almost everything a traveller might need to know about that country, from food to protocol and camels to dervishes. One of the highlights of the branch's early history has to be the part it played in the diplomatic success in the Congress of Berlin in which Disraeli had faced a potential war with Russia, but he came home and made his famous statement that the nation had 'peace with honour'. Following this, the Secretary for India, Salisbury, wrote that the Intelligence Department of the War Office had played a major part in the success of the 'preceding diplomatic negotiations'.

It is arguably Wolseley's modus operandi regarding his staff that formed the most important influence on what eventually turned out to be the efficient central 'engine room' of the new branch. After all, in the 1870s he had Brackenbury with him as well as Maurice. Brackenbury typified this approach, in which the commander took time to select the right man for each particular role in his team. As Wolseley's biographer has written: 'Henry Brackenbury would never have gained appointment on either his looks or social gifts. In uniform he appeared to be a businessman in disguise.'[72] But what Wolseley saw was that side of Brackenbury with his special talent for articulating the bearing of theory on practice warfare. The man the team called 'Brack' developed into a hard worker and a superbly gifted organizer – very much what we now think of as a personal assistant. But he was not always sitting at a desk or taking notes: he was one of the first men to walk into Esaman in the Ashanti campaign.

John Frederick Maurice, as previously explained, came to prominence in the Ashanti campaigns. Intelligence in all forms became his province, and Wolseley was to prize him very highly. When Maurice was wounded in the action against Sekukuni in November 1879, Wolseley wrote to Mrs Maurice: 'Your most gallant husband has been wounded in the left shoulder, but not badly. He is as chirpy as possible and like a good soldier, makes nothing of his wound.' He went on to say that 'I am proud to count your husband amongst those whom I regard as my bravest companions in arms and most sincere friends.'[73]

Maurice was born in 1841 and studied at Addiscombe College and at Woolwich Academy. He joined the Royal Artillery in 1861. After the southern African experience he was Deputy Adjutant General in the campaign against Arabi in Egypt in 1882. Arguably his real talent was in the theoretical aspects of military intelligence, and he was a professor at the Staff College from 1885 to 1892. At the beginning of his active career with the Ashanti he had written a preparatory text on the history, culture and topography of the people and the land, and he was to write a history of that war in 1874. He wrote a wide-ranging history of the Anglo-Boer War between 1906 and 1910.

Maurice was always the person Wolseley was most likely to consult in matters of military intelligence; in 1895, writing from the Royal Hospital in Dublin, Wolseley was concerned about the aspects of intelligence existing outside the staff on a campaign, and he wrote to Maurice about his position on this: 'Without putting yourself to any trouble can you tell me where to find some good sound denunciation of the Indian system of putting political agents to control generals in the field?' He asked his friend if he had any knowledge of instances in which diplomatic agents had interfered with generals in the course of a campaign.

This was something at the heart of the system since India had been developed and controlled: residents of the East India Company, accustomed to running vast territories more by diplomacy than hard steel and fear, and also local magistrates, had found that profound cultural knowledge and linguistic skills had achieved incredible security and success.

Maurice was in agreement with his tutor, but was tactful; Wolseley was ill at the time and tended to let obsessions get hold of him. Their friendship was deep, enduring and important to both.

JOHN DUNN

John Dunn, born in 1834, was of the second generation of settlers who went to colonize the Eastern Cape in 1820. His father, Robert Dunn, had married Anne Biggar, the daughter of a veteran of the Napoleonic Wars, Alexander Biggar, in 1824. Around the years 1838–1842, Robert Dunn is notable in Natal for being a trader and then an 'agent' for Britain. He had lived over the bay in a place called Sea View.

John was just fourteen when his father died and he found work as a guide and a hunter. One of the keenest insights into Dunn's character is his friendship with Sikonyana, who had run from his tribe in Zululand after falling in love with a girl who had not been given permission to marry him by King Mpande. The couple was captured by the border agent, Joshua Walmsley, known as Mashonga. At the time he became friendly with Sikonyana, Dunn was working for Walmsley as an interpreter. Later, when Dunn had land in Zululand, Sikonyana became one of Dunn's district headmen.

This tells us a great deal about why Dunn was so useful to the British, of course. His abilities are outstandingly illustrated in the case of a Zulu fugitive called Mlandela, who, before Dunn was in Zululand, had land in the British reserve. He set about stealing some of Dunn's cattle. What then happened is described by A T Bryant, who had been a missionary in the area after 1879: 'That was an error, for this John Dunn was a mighty Nimrod, fearless alike of lions, bees and Tongas [a tribe] … Dunn, with a force of 2,000 native levies at once marched into Mtetwaland … the rebel Mtetwa were routed and chased pell-mell as far as the Mfolozi river …'

Dunn's time with Walmsley was very important as a formative period in his life. It was largely because of his work with Walmsley, leading parties into Zululand and learning to be a guide, that increased his regional knowledge, of course. It was after a particularly violent and dangerous episode in Dunn's life that he moved into Zululand, a close associate of Cetshwayo. In 1856 Mpande and Prince Mbuyazi were at loggerheads over the royal succession and Mbuyazi ran to Natal, wanting help from the border authorities. This was Walmsley's province and he had to find a way to avoid the conflict escalating. The armies of Cetshwayo were coming to face the renegade and some traders were trapped in the middle of the conflict.

Dunn offered to go and try either to find a settlement of the issues or to fight. He only just escaped from what became a fierce confrontation; Mbuyazi's men ran for it and the opposition were out for slaughter. Dunn was caught up in all this, and writing about it later he said, 'I was besieged from all sides by men clinging to me, so that my horse … was completely rooted to the spot. I now jumped off, stripped myself … and taking nothing but my gun … swam with one hand.' There was a massacre of Mbuyazi's followers.[74]

But Dunn had been noticed by the Zulu King and he was invited to be Cetshwayo's diplomat in the affairs of power games with the British and the Boers. Dunn accepted the offer and married a Zulu woman, although he had married Catherine Pierce in 1853. The hunter and guide then became, to all intents and purposes, a Zulu chief.

In terms of Dunn's movements and thinking after the setbacks of early 1879, the story is one of duplicity on his part when seen through Zulu eyes, but with a more distant and objective stance this was *Realpolitik*. After all, he was a man with power and status, like any chief with a tribe. Chelmsford, well behind the battle positions, had, of course, survived the January of horrors for the army. In the phase of the war after Isandlwana, when the tide turned, it was in part due to the activities of Dunn. Dunn had actually been made an ally of Cetshwayo some time earlier, being given the task of liaising with and supervising the various white settlers and visitors to the area of Zululand along the coast. Dunn's family was in Port Natal, but he went closer to being a hybrid, absorbing the native culture to a large extent. He had swayed back and forth across the two cultures and in a civil war between Zulu leaders he chose the wrong one and was almost killed. But to all intents and purposes he was a general with Cetshwayo. He it was who obtained weapons for Cetshwayo and he became the main intelligence source regarding the British when trouble was brewing.

But when it came to reprisals after Isandlwana, and Chelmsford needed information, Dunn had re-crossed the line. It was due to Chelmsford that Dunn became an ally. His involvement was highly significant, as he had a corps of spies who could venture into the interior easily and with a sense of normality. Donald Morris has written an account of when and where Dunn sided with Chelmsford:

> On the twenty-first of February the General was riding back to Durban from a visit to Fort Pearson, when he encountered a smart gig driving north. John Dunn, the unhappy occupant, had been dreading this meeting … Dunn was well aware that the war could only have one outcome, and he naturally hope to return to Zululand once the war was over … Chelmsford now forced him off the fence. Chelmsford was sufficiently sympathetic to his problem not to force him to accept an official post … and when the troops entered Zululand John Dunn marched at the head of 244 armed retainers, officially listed as the Head of Intelligence.[75]

In the buildup to the fight at Eshowe, Dunn formed units of supporting fighters, and when the time was right he supplied a detailed report on the situation in Zululand for Chelmsford from material originally gathered by a spy, Magumbi. As has been described, the report gave very specific information about where the enemy was placed and in what numbers. Magumbi estimated that in the area in which Chelmsford was to move, there were some definite indications that some of the army that had been around at Isandlwana had moved north. It became a matter of some urgency to move on to the offensive. Chelmsford knew from the reports that his best route was close to the coast; he then could predict more or less where he would be most likely to be attacked. This time he knew what the problems linked to moving supplies and arms would be and he put special attention on that issue. It was also not absolutely certain that the report from Magumbi could be trusted, so there was caution in every small move from then on. But as he advanced, aware of Zulu scouts, he was attentive to messages from border agents. The column stayed together; at the Nyezane a force of about 11,000 Zulu had gathered to meet the column. The odds were now two to one and there was no dispersal of British forces. Chelmsford knew that he had a relief column behind him and he laagered the column to meet the Zulu attack. It was a case of traditional defence and rifle-fire. This time the Zulu retreated and threw away weapons in panic.

How much of the success at Eshowe was down to John Dunn and his agents? Arguably, a great deal is the answer. Dunn, who rode beside the staff some of the time, actually fired at Dabulamanzi, his former ally, as the fight receded. He had become a turncoat, of course, but he was a pragmatist who wanted his lifestyle to continue in the place he loved, and he sided with the winners. His network of spies had played a major part in the turning of the tide against the Zulu. Credit must be given to Chelmsford as well, in having to cope with a plethora of information. In one report he notes: 'The report of Mr Fynney is diametrically opposed to that which I have received from the border commanders during my numerous visits to that part of the country …'[76]

It was down to John Dunn also that the pockets of Zulu power in the coastal strip were suppressed. In all the work of the Eshowe relief column Dunn rode with them, along with his scouts. He had been in Zululand since 1853 and knew it very well, as no British officer could have done. The official Army Records Society volume on the war notes that Dunn was accused of treachery by Cetshwayo's advisers, and that it was in late 1878 that he 'threw in his lot with the British'. If so, we can only regret that he was not active in the party that left Rorke's Drift on that fateful day when the column moved towards Isandlwana. He had a good life, and lived until 1895, leaving behind 49 wives and 117 children. It might well be asked whether any of his sons continued his work and made a living spying for the government. In fact, none did. Many of his daughters married Europeans, and they settled down in Dunn's land, but the family scattered far and wide.

We have an insight into this man, who eventually inherited about a third of Zululand, from the memoirs of Robert Baden-Powell, who was with General Smyth later. In 1888 Dunn was to fight Cetshwayo's son, Dinuzulu, and by that time Dunn had 48 Zulu wives and over 100 children. Baden-Powell met him and noted that he was 'a fine broad-shouldered bearded man of middle age wearing a cowboy hat and an Inverness cloak, and carrying a rifle'. He had a force of 2,000 Zulus behind him then, and Baden-Powell was impressed, writing, 'When we topped the rise we saw moving up towards us from the valley below three long lines of men marching in single file and singing a wonderful anthem as they marched.' As Tim Jeal has said in his biography of Baden-Powell, 'When he one day wrote choruses for his Boy Scouts and dreamed up campfire rituals, John Dunn's Zulus would be in the forefront of his mind.' [77]

Dunn became a very powerful man, and given the differences in his immediate cultural environment, it would not be inaccurate to describe him as a country gentlemen – but with a very different kind of hunting and shooting on offer. The clearest description we have of him comes from Bertram Mitford, a traveller, who noted his strong build and regular features, reporting on his 'weather-tanned countenance' and 'plain tweed suit'.

Naturally, Dunn was in an increasingly perilous and difficult position in terms of the necessary diplomacy required to maintain a neutral stance, but as matters accelerated towards the end of 1878 he obviously began to realize that he would have to return to his British allegiances. But his reasons were broader than that, as he himself explained, when he wrote that his father had suffered by remaining neutral, and also that he could be useful 'in averting another disaster'. He must have known that his land and buildings left behind in Zululand would be vulnerable and, of course, the Zulus destroyed them.

Ian Knight has pointed out that during Dunn's travels with Chelmsford's column there was a very unfortunate event when Dunn's scouts were mistakenly thought to be the enemy. Despite shouts of friendship, there was carnage, and Knight points out that Dunn found one of his men dead, with a bayonet wound in his chest. This happened at eMvutsheni and Knight explains that it started when 'a shot fired by a nervous piquet caused a mad scramble for the safety of the laager …'[78]

One interesting sidelight on Dunn comes in an anecdote from General Sir Arthur Cunynghame, who tells of Dunn being present when a Dr Drummond was summoned to King Cetshwayo in order to help treat the King's sick wife. The doctor prescribed oysters and porter for the sick woman and this appears to have been efficacious; Cetshwayo awarded 300 head of cattle to the medical man, but Dunn had already made a private agreement for just 100 to be given. In addition to that difficult diplomatic position, Cunynghame reports that Dunn was also Cetshwayo's 'poison taster' – something very difficult to believe.[79]

John Dunn, as his descendent Daniel Dunn wrote, was 'unique in southern Africa's historical annals for a he founded a distinct new community … Yet John Dunn unknowingly bequeathed a bitter sweet legacy to his descendants. The distribution of John Dunn's property was immediately cloned with dispute.'[80]

He died in 1895, suffering from dropsy and heart disease, after a short illness.

HENRY FRANCIS FYNN

Fynn was a colonist, born in the Cape Colony in 1846, the son of Henry Fynn, who had gone out to Natal with the same generation as Robert Dunn in 1824. As was the case with Dunn, Fynn was immersed in the Zulu culture and tribal establishment and he was with Shepstone in 1873 when the sham coronation of Cetshwayo took place. He then became magistrate in the Msinga district.

Fynn figures prominently in Chelmsford's correspondence and plans after February 1879. He had already filled the place of interpreter in the negotiations of December 1878 and as a conflict became more and more certain he was in demand as a military adviser. Such workings of intelligence were common in India, when political officers and regional magistrates provided the essential knowledge of the language and mindset of specific tribes or people, and in southern Africa the use of Fynn in this way is a sure indication that, eventually, Natal and its British forces were going to be shocked into falling in line with the Army of India in these matters. Basically, as Chelmsford had problems with his staff and openly admitted that he needed more officers with intelligence skills or sources than he had available, Fynn was attached almost as a member of the staff 'team'.

After Isandlwana – where Fynn had arrived after the battle – his main impact on events was in his organization of the Border patrols. In the month after Isandlwana he supervised these positions, personally visiting them and offering support. He later played an important part in the diplomatic manoeuvres with the Zulus along the border, attempting to settle matters peacefully, but without the knowledge of the defeat at Ulundi, this was slow and uncertain. Nevertheless, by late August, peace was ratified and Fynn was there to accept the submission of most of the leaders of the Zulus in that area. He represents that type of figure in the war whose expertise was essential and whose communication skills were equally impressive. As with Dunn, he was seen as a quasi-staff entity, with a respected status.

Fynn was still there when Cetshwayo returned to settle in the by then emasculated kingdom and obviously the diplomatic tasks involved were almost impossible to accomplish, and the civil war of 1883 ended his efforts to try to have an impact on some kind of resolution there. Fynn died in Pietermaritzburg in 1915.

HENRY LONGCAST

Longcast was another invaluable interpreter and sage on Zulu affairs and language. He was born in 1850 and was put in an orphanage with his sister after the death of their parents. Later they were adopted by a missionary working in Zululand: a mission station was permitted to be established by King Mpande in 1857. Like Dunn, Longcast then gathered respect and status with the Zulus as he grew older and learned their ways. He came to know not only Cetshwayo, but other famous leaders such as Sihayo and Dabulamanzi. It is hard to underestimate his contribution to the third stage of the war, when the tide turned in favour of Britain.

Robert Robinson, the missionary, stood with Frere on the expansionist ideology: he supported invasion and colonization, so as the situation worsened in late 1877 Robertson left. Longcast remained until close to the outbreak of hostilities. With his background, consequently he had the kind of knowledge required for an army with no reliable maps and no official Intelligence Branch documentation on the terrain. Longcast knew the country, and up to the battle at Ulundi he was extremely useful to Chelmsford. He stayed in place when Wolseley took over and was with Gifford when in pursuit of Cetshwayo, and after the capture of the King Longcast was clearly the best person to remain with the captive, for both protection and information. He and Cetshwayo were friendly until the troubles of 1883. He died in 1908 while travelling home, after seeing his life decline through poverty and the loss of his former land in Zululand.

Characters such as Longcast illustrate the reliance of the British command on amateurs for essential knowledge. From the very start, Chelmsford knew, as he must have done in the previous Frontier War, that assembling all kinds of knowledge of natives and topography was the first step in having a successful intelligence staff. But that was never a priority, and the assumptions made were done with a belief in traditional methods of attack and a certainty that in the field the Martini-Henry would win every time against stabbing spears and raw courage.

8

Correspondents, Media and Knowledge

In the Crimean War, the Tsar of Russia claimed to obtain all the intelligence about the British military he needed from the pages of *The Times*. That may have been an exaggeration, but the essence of the statement reveals an uncomfortable truth: the media in the Victorian years provided masses of information on war, as they did on everything else. The turning point was arguably the Crimean War and the reporting of William Howard Russell of *The Times*. He had seen much of the action in the Crimea, spending almost two years there.

One of the soldiers at the front described him as a great smoker and drinker and added that he was just the chap to get information. His influence may be gauged from the fact that Lord Raglan disliked him and his adverse effect on morale. His dispatches home were a landmark in war reporting, particularly after the Battle of the Alma in 1854 and later of Sevastopol. He went to India after the 1857 Mutiny, and in his book on that journey he writes in his preface what amounts to an essay on the knowledge and power of the war correspondent by that time. He wrote: 'My creed is that we never can hold India by the sword but at a cost of money which England cannot afford to pay, and that any attempt to diminish the expenditure by large employment of native agency is certainly dangerous, and will probably be unsuccessful.'[82] There he writes like an officer or military attaché with opinions on what should or could be the basis for intelligence work. There is a massive assumption beneath that statement: he takes for granted that an amateur and a civilian may have an informed opinion on military affairs. He wrote from a time in which the first mass media, the national press, was beginning to exert influence on all aspects of life. Not only did he bring the realities of war home to domestic readers, but he also, by simply going out to the front, provided a template for military knowledge that was to proliferate. The war correspondent, particularly when photography had come along to join forces with the pen, was by the 1850s a person with a very high status who might move in the same circles as officers, civil servants and politicians; the writer in this context knew about war as the soldier knew it. That applies to the Zulu War in particular.

By 1879 the top-level journalists and documentary writers had attained a 'star' identity; the hack writer was still there, but some press people were becoming celebrities. Popular writers for the press had their own demarcated areas of expertise, as Matthew Sweet explains:

> Ida Wells Barnet, for instance, was an African American journalist who bought an interest in the Memphis Free Speech newspaper and made a long career out of tackling issues of racial inequality, often putting herself in danger to do so. Winifred Sweet Black was a hard-boiled political reporter who hid under a table in President Benjamin Harrison's railroad car in order to obtain an interview ...[82]

Russell was not alone, then, in his brazen and sometimes pompous opinions on matters that were really for the military profession to consider. He was one of a new breed, writers who saw no contradiction in legislating opinion on grand and consequential affairs of state or policy abroad.

An important point about Russell and *The Times* is the impact of the editor, John Delane, and his attitudes to correspondents. During the Crimean War a correspondent called Thomas Chenery was expressing nothing but the opinions of the ambassador in Turkey, giving a party line. Delane wrote to reprimand him and complained that Chenery was asserting that Britain wished to lose all its interests and claims. Delane threatened to sack his man at the front.

The War Office of course realized the dangers in this power potentially outside their domain. After the reporting of the disastrous retreat from Kabul in 1842, there was a gradual tightening of regulations with regard to the status and control of correspondents. As so often happened in the Victorian army, the dictat first came from the Indian Press Commissioner, backed by the Intelligence Branch of the Quartermaster General's Department in the Horse Guards. Intelligence was centred there in the decades before the 1873 establishment. The statement on the issue was presented in Simla in 1870 and had a long list of intended controls, the main ones being:

> (a) All correspondents desiring to write for newspapers at the seat of war must be furnished with a licence granted under the authority of the Government of India. The Licence shall state the paper or papers to which the correspondent is agent.
>
> (b) On no account may a correspondent write for other papers than those mentioned on his licence ...
>
> (c) No-one may write for a newspaper without a licence. The Government of India will not grant licences to those whom they consider undesirable to have as correspondents in the field. Retired officers will be preferred.[83]

Of course, writers were well aware of the intelligence issues related to what they were doing. Archibald Forbes discussed this in an article written in 1880, and he dismissed the impact on actual field knowledge, referring to his southern African experience: 'Ketchwayo [sic] was reported to take in the Natal Witness, but the nimble runner who brought him a stale copy of that print could wipe the eye of its out of date "latest intelligence" by the information gathered by his own powers of observation.'[84] Forbes faces up to the basic question: is there any negative factor in the operations of correspondents with regard to a specific theatre of war? He plainly states his view with regard to the conditions of imperial warfare as he knew it in his time:

> There is vastly more weight in the objection that the war correspondent with his head loose may give information to the

> enemy. It is, however, obvious that this objection can only have weight were it possible that his information can reach that enemy; in other words, where a modicum of civilisation and accessibility is the attribute of your enemy.[85]

In the colonial wars the 'uncivilized' enemy was almost always one which attacked and confronted, and that usually speedily. Exceptions may be found in India, and that again explains why the regulations against correspondents were issued there. Forbes was quite right to assert that, apart from the Crimea, the enemies of the Crown had been such that only quick and efficient field intelligence was likely to impact on results, and in that regard war correspondents were marginal to matters of tactics. Yet there was always a shadowy presence of localized intelligence behind the lines. In the case of the Zulu War that came from all possible civilian quarters: missionaries, magistrates, travellers, academics and administrators were potential sources of productive and relevant information about the Zulus. Fynney and Dunn provided profiles of the Zulu war machine – and added the cultural and religious factors which had a bearing on their fighting. But there was nothing in reverse that compared with that. The Zulu counterpart was real, grounded espionage, behind the lines, as will be related in the next chapter.

Forbes, however, did admit in his essay that there was an element of risk in the presence of the correspondent, and he saw this in the case study of the Russo-Turkish War at Kars. Russia declared war on Turkey in April 1877. Forbes himself had reported on that siege in the Plevna campaign in December 1877. In his essay he recalled that

> I have known evil done. One journal, during the recent Russo-Turkish War, published wholly unjustifiable details of the defences of Kars and its information was naturally taken advantage of by the assailants of that fortress. Another journal published, from its correspondent, particulars of the defence of Rustchuck …'[86]

The Forbes essay weighs and considers the pros and cons of allowing correspondents a degree of freedom within the war they are covering. In the context of the Zulu War, Forbes took a very active part and

Sepoy Zulu soldiers, from the *Daily Graphic* 1890

Zulu warrior, from a documentary survey of 1900 (author's collection)

Wolseley (as satirised in *Punch*, the supreme administrator)

Sketch of a helioscope (Royal Signals Museum, monograph)

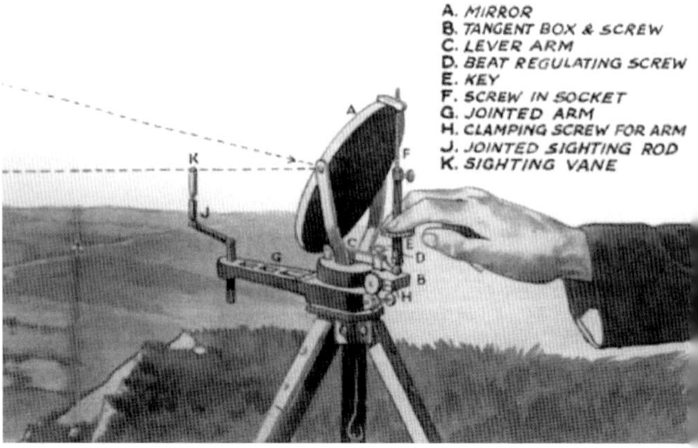

Sketch of action at Hlobane
(Stanley Wood, 1895)

Plan of the Battle of Khambula
(*Battles of the Nineteenth Century*)

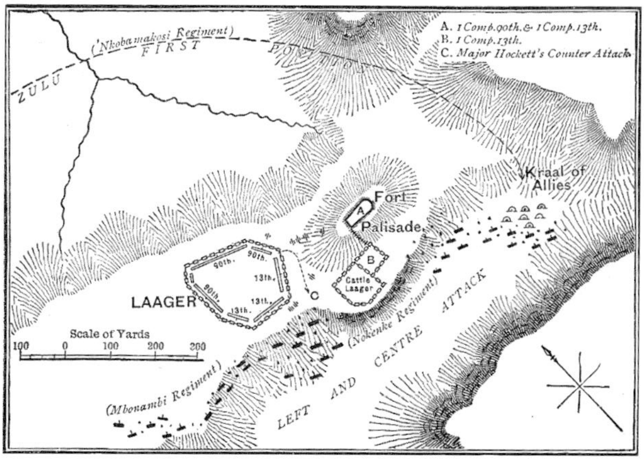

Sketch of the mounted rifles in action,
Ulundi (Stanley Wood, 1895)

Sir Evelyn Wood (*Battles of the Nineteenth Century*)

Sir Henry Brtle Frere
(Alan Bott, *Our Fathers* 1900)

John Dunn (courtesy of Adrian Greaves and Ian Knight)

Sitshitshili (courtesy of Adrian Greaves and Ian Knight)

Ntshingwayo Ka Mahole (courtesy of Adrian Greaves and Ian Knight)

Keith Johnston, geographer
(*Illustrated London News* 1879)

Map of Fort Pearson and Eshowe (from the 1880 *Narrative of the Field Operations of the Zulu War*)

Officers reading a map (Prior, in *Illustrated London News* 1879)

Looking for Spies after the death of the Prince Imperial (*Illustrated London News* 1879)

The sketch of the helioscope drawn by Prior (*Illustrated London News* 1879)

Zulu Spy in the grass (*Illustrated London News* 1879)

The Charge of the 17th lancers at Ulundi
(Alan Bott, *Our Fathers* 1900)

General Newdigate interrogating a Zulu spy at his HQ, Landsman's Drift (*Illustrated London News* 1879)

Military Ballooning (*Illustrated London News* 1879)

famously rode swiftly with the news of Isandlwana to his telegraph point. But of course, in 1879 the telegraph had not reached Capetown. It ended at Madeira, hence the long delay in news from the war reaching London. That delay had allowed Frere the time he needed to work his diplomacy towards a war with plenty of time and space for ignoring orders from Hicks Beach in London, and Forbes had the problem in reverse.

Most significant for present purposes is Forbes' critique of Chelmsford. If the new breed of writers were figures assuming great sway over public opinion, then they were in competition with the generals and ministers in terms of speaking with authority on a particular conflict. The article Forbes wrote and Chelmsford's response are of profound interest for the subject of war correspondents and their place vis-à-vis military intelligence.

Forbes expressed most of the points discussed in chapter 4 but of course Chelmsford was singled out, as he was at home in the press. Robert Blake has summarized the opinions at home:

> The defeat of Isandlwana caused an outcry in England for the supersession of both Frere and Chelmsford. There was something to be said for bowing to the storm and recalling them at the earliest moment. There was more to be said … for backing them to the full and allowing them to redeem their blunder, if such it was …[87]

Clearly, a little later, Ulundi had eclipsed Isandlwana to many commentators and to the public, but Chelmsford's responses to the criticism have to be understood in the context of the flak he had taken before Forbes wrote the critique.

In the Queen's household, the shock of Princess Alice's death on 14 December 1878 was closely followed by the news from Africa, and one immediate consequence of this was that the planned marriage of Prince Arthur was postponed. That general depression coloured the responses to the news of Chelmsford's disaster. Both Victoria and her friend and governor to Prince Arthur, Sir Howard Elphinstone of the Crimean War fame, saw errors and puzzles in the events of Isandlwana: 'The defeat was the greatest humiliation for the British army in living memory … Afterwards, Durnford was posthumously castigated for failing to defend the camp. Even the Queen wondered how it was that Durnford had been enticed away during the action.'[88]

There were voices in defence of Chelmsford also: all kinds of military men offered explanations, perhaps most typical was that of Colonel William Fielding who wrote from the United Services Club to stress how many people had no real understanding of 'the general commanding an expedition on active service'. Fielding explained that after planning, the general's chief concern is 'to screen his own movements and to hide his plan of campaign from his enemy; while he learns from his most trusted officers, through scouting parties the positions, forces and plans of his adversaries'. Fielding then emphasizes what has since been generally thought – that Chelmsford had inadequate field intelligence, and there was no personal blame attached after Isandlwana.[89]

In defending himself against the accusations of Forbes, in a memorandum of February 1880, Chelmsford left historians of the future a very clear apologia for actions taken. One paragraph in particular surely states the principal reason for defeat, and consequently provides the position from which Forbes wrote:

> I have already mentioned that for military purpose the information regarding the character of the country was of little value, and it is clear that no reconnaissances could be made into Zululand until after war was declared – and therefore 'no such provision' was 'within the scope of the military art' at the time when it was needed.[90]

This much-discussed memo from Chelmsford opens up most of the important issues with regard to the war correspondents in this war. There were three main writers from England in this context: Forbes, Charles Norris-Newman and Melton Prior. But there were also many writers from the Natal papers. Few wars have been so thoroughly reported – in this case very much by locals in the Natal newspapers as well as by Forbes and Norris-Newman. In terms of how they related to the fluid intelligence of this war, the central point is that they were supportive of the British officer and they tried to understand his viewpoint on things. In the end, their purpose was to produce copy that would be exciting and dramatic to read – narratives that would form part of the ongoing story of how the Empire was being won and retained.

Along with the writers came the special artists: notably Melton Prior of *The Illustrated London News* and Charles Fripp of *The Graphic*. Visual records are especially important in the history of military intelligence, in the localized area of work, because they had a documentary aspect in the Victorian age. Artists were particularly open to being accused of espionage, as in the case of war artist William Simpson, famous for his work in the Crimea, who was arrested in Germany at Metz in 1870 on suspicion of being a spy. Most drawings give detailed and accurate images of warriors and battle scenes, terrain and resources. They were the kinds of notations that had been done for decades by the writer-travellers into Asia. Charles Norris-Newman's work also has a significance in this documentary aspect: he was there from the start of Chelmsford's advance, being attached to the third Natal Native Contingent in the Third Column. His writing and the illustrations in his book, *In Zululand with the British Throughout the War of 1879*, exemplifies the best elements of the documentary method in that age of fact-gathering. He wastes no time in that work in offering a concise explanation of the weakness in the campaign: 'They, however, greatly miscalculated the power of their new foe.'[91]

Forbes was the successor to Russell in that he was the top man in status and in authority, but Norris-Newman was there first in Zululand, as he wrote in his book: 'I was the first and only correspondent in the field with the troops … Having been sometime previously residing in Natal I knew something of the country …'[92] After Isandlwana, though, he was certainly not the only reporter there; other nationals took an interest and *The London Standard* sent F R MacKenzie, Forbes came for *The Daily News* and William Peace wrote for the *Daily Telegraph*.

Forbes, born in 1838, surely takes the limelight in this war for sheer bravado, enterprise and personality. He had some army experience, serving as an ordinary soldier in the Royal Dragoons, but he became interested in the theory of warfare after being invalided out of the army in 1867. In some ways he represents the same kind of attitude as the novelist H Rider Haggard: adding mythic and glamorous dimensions to the dirty business of killing. But there is no denying his determination and experience as his career stood in 1879: he had reported from the Russo-Turkish War and the Afghan War, and such was his image that he was as interesting to his readers as the most dashing characters he celebrated – men like Colonel Fred Burnaby, who was to die heroically at Abu Klea in the Sudan in 1885.

Forbes' impact on how the Zulu War was understood and placed into the popular imagination, even a generation later, was not limited to his journalism, but reached works of popular history. In the year of his death, 1900, his name was still in such works on battles and great commanders issued by the mass market press, with the name Forbes being alongside that of novelists such as G A Henty. The 1890s saw the rise of the novelists who specialized in male adventure in the great narrative of Empire. Forbes' name was there with them, a part of that enterprise coinciding with the Anglo-Boer War and the victory of Omdurman.[93]

The significance of the war correspondents at this time was that they informed the public on all aspects of a campaign, even writing copy as events and decisions were in progress, as in this writing for the *Natal Mercury*, printed a few days after Isandlwana: 'The events of this week fully bear out all that the oldest colonists have said and urged regarding Zulu tactics. In both cases they have attacked what they no doubt deemed the weakest columns ...'[94] This confirms what servants of the Empire across the world had learned for decades, against all kinds of foes: localized intelligence is the knowledge of prime importance.

What was happening, then, is that through the writing of the correspondents and other media later, the events in the Zulu War were being described and analyzed largely as a case study and an object lesson in what not to do. From the viewpoint of the command and the staff, an offensive made total sense: the problem was with the nature of the enemy and the lack of any consistent and reliable information. Of course, it seemed at the time, as the invasion of Zululand took place, that the usual approaches would do very nicely: the correspondents and other commentators saw the failings.

Men such as Forbes and Norris-Newman were an integral part of that ongoing progress towards establishing a proper, organized and integrated corpus of resources and information on the various peoples of the earth and their military mindset and tactics. Forbes and Norris-Newman, in an important sense, witnessed the limitations of close planning and communications in the face of a vast terrain and an unacknowledged enemy. Assumptions about the enemy, based on previous opposition who were thought to be of a similar disposition and nature, were disastrously wrong-headed and the correspondents saw this. This is why, over the next twenty years, there was an emergence of a new class of writers on military affairs – correspondents with a deep interest in theory and tactics: men such as G W Steevens, in *With Kitchener to Khartoum* (1898). Like Forbes, Steevens wrote books on the problems of the military presence in the Empire, but more than that, he went into Europe at dangerous times and was arrested as a spy in Austria.

The years after the Zulu War saw an increase in such intellectual stances on warfare, yet these were still fused with the spirit of Forbes and Norris-Newman. The knowledge supplied by war correspondents was to become valuable to the Intelligence Branch, as had the writings of gentleman amateurs who had travelled to Africa to hunt or to collect specimens of flora and fauna.

The name of the game in 1879 with regard to intelligence work was what we now call 'humint' – the kind of information that involves people. In other words, fluid intelligence, communication and factual data delivered without a necessarily reliable or known source. Information for Chelmsford was taken from men in the field, colonists, missionaries, and of course from discussions with staff who already knew the area and the opposition – men such as Cunynghame. The fact is that, in African contexts, the previous enemies of imperial troops had been less than impressive, but the Zulus were a totally different proposition.

One of the best sources we have for how Cetshwayo operated his spies is in the memoirs of Cunynghame. In that he gives a full summary of the activities of his spies behind the British lines:

> Upon arrival in Pretoria we exchanged our clothes for blue serge coats and trousers, obtained from a retired policeman. Upon consultation we determined to wait until her Majesty's birthday. We had no difficulty in obtaining work in Pretoria, being old hands, and understanding a little English and Dutch, picked up on the diamond fields. We were surprised to find such a large dorp in the interior, but found every store belonged to Englishmen, as all the people talked against the late government; therefore we consider there was no chance of fighting and our mission was at an end. Her Majesty's birthday passed off very orderly. Much to our disappointment, we noticed very few Boers, but hoped they would show up with their generals and attack the redcoats, scattered all over the hills. We came to the conclusion that British infantry look very well at play, but doubt their abilities in bush country – we could, for instance, massacre in five minutes that little body in our country. We were much impressed by the rapidity of the artillery; they were well backed up by those ferocious-looking fellows, the mounted police, who reports say are regular blood-suckers and would prove to be very tough customers to us. We suppose Somtsen [Shepstone Senior] had his Mabutos out to frighten the Boers – they had on their talismans of war. We did not see the late president, we hear he was afraid. Sir T Shepstone intended sending him to the island where Langalabalele is under the escort of the blood suckers.
>
> We tried to get a look at the machine which they say is iawa inblamusi [the Gatling gun] but the building and street corner were always watched by some ugly fellows who we were told had just returned from murdering Sekokone's women.
>
> We also noticed the induna from Swaziland and his followers. We tried hard on several occasions to pump him on their mission but without much effect, but we are sure that they are now English ...

There are several points of interest here. First, it is noticeable that these spies moved freely around and asked lots of questions. Despite the fact that they were in the uniforms of police officers, and so would not have stood out in any way, they appear to have been curious on matters for which they would be assumed to have been informed about. In other words, these men must have known how to work discreetly, like proper, skilled agents undercover. The British had no counterparts in that respect, and that says everything about the humint differences between the opposing armies.

These spies clearly had a list of objectives in their briefing – a quest as sophisticated as anything of a similar nature that might have occurred in a European war. Most impressive of all is surely the communication skills hinted at beneath the references to the various targets of their mission. They are aware of all the elements here, not simply military details but also social and communal differences and identities. Why else would they remark on the English being the shopkeepers? They also provide what every commander prays for: assessments of the temperament and disposition of the enemy. The consequences of their assessment of the redcoats is foreboding in its tone, with later disasters in mind: as Kipling said in a poem not long after the 1879 conflict, the Zulu *impis* 'dished us up in style'.[95]

Cunynghame, recalling this from oral sources, notes the problems he personally had in having anything like this kind of resource. He notes: 'One of my greatest difficulties was in the intelligence department, which appears to have been sadly neglected …' He adds that native policemen could have had the necessary potential to perhaps undertake such work, but that it was never going to happen.[96] The confidence behind this secret embassy into the enemy stronghold is greatly impressive. Thirty years later, in Baden-Powell's *Scouting for Boys*, elements of that Zulu culture which lay behind such achievements were incorporated into the scouting ideas, such as the shape of the wood badges, copying those of the *isiqu* beads of the Zulu King Dinuzulu. Baden-Powell recognized the excellence of Zulu espionage and field scouting and gave it full recognition. As the founder of the Scouts commented in the same book, 'The native boys of the Zulu and the Swazi tribes learn to be scouts before they are allowed to be considered men' and he tells the tale of the warrior painted white and cast out in the bush to survive, making the point that if he is caught while white, he has failed.[97] There may be some exaggeration here, but the point is that Baden-

Powell, as a scout in real war, confirmed the Zulu ability, seeing that their military culture stood out in that respect. In 1888 he had been aide-de-camp to Sir Henry Smyth in Zululand, and used that knowledge in his lectures and writings on field intelligence to staff long before writing on scouting for younger readers.

It is obvious from this report that Cetshwayo had a cadre of tried and tested undercover spies; he had scouts in the undulating hills who could do reconnaissance on every step of progression of invading armies, and because Chelmsford's columns moved so slowly, with their burdens of ox-carts and provisions, he knew his enemy's position as well as his disposition. The behind-the-line spying is one marker placing the Zulus well ahead of the British army at the time in this respect.

This is all 'humint' – and the war correspondents knew about this. From the Crimea twenty years earlier, Russell and others had gathered enough knowledge to know that Britain could easily be placed at a perilous disadvantage in a battle at the level of humint and at the level of tactics based on intelligence. It was only to be expected, then, that after 1879 the war correspondent became rather more than that, becoming in many cases a civilian branch of the intelligence establishment in the army. If theoretical intelligence was not professionalized and monopolized in the Staff College and in the army high command, then amateurs would butt in. If we compare the army with the Bar at that time, the difference is stunningly informative. A barrister or solicitor was part of an elite and had a vocabulary and a ritual to follow; a layman would not have presumed to pass an opinion on affairs at, say, Gray's Inn or in the office of the Home Secretary. But in military affairs, if a man in the imperial wars failed once and it was momentous, then generally the stain was there and the failure public. The press, the growing third estate of power, was becoming a prominent source of military information by the 1870s and the Anglo-Zulu War was a wake-up call to the leading men in the army at Whitehall.

A massive paradox with this in mind is that humint was integral to the wars in Africa, but often secondary to texts and handbooks in the Indian conflicts. Yet again, southern Africa was becoming more than a case study in failure and compromise: it was a template of mistakes and errors, something to use in the theory lessons when officers played the war games and explained formative ill-conceived strategies. As Forbes said in his assessment of how correspondents related to the officer class: 'how has it come about that, not a few times, the scientific elite of our military service have crowded into the lecture hall of the United Services Institution to listen to lectures from war correspondents, on the abstrusest technicalities of the strategy and tactics of foreign armies?'[98]

9

The Empire, Intelligence and the Zulu Experience

When Lord Chelmsford responded to Forbes' criticism in his memorandum of February 1880, he wrote: 'Sir Bartle and myself were both fully impressed with the gravity of the situation, and the extreme probability which existed of a serious raid of Zulus being made into natal or the Transvaal.' He was following one of the secondary repercussions of the Forward Policy of the current imperialists, of whom Frere was a prominent member. But Chelmsford also localized matters, adding,

> The peculiar nature of the Natal and Transvaal border, its great extent and the fewness of the troops to watch it, rendered to my mind any attempt to defend it directly almost impossible, and I came to the conclusion, the accuracy of which I still maintain, that the best chance of saving the two colonies from the consequences of such an inroad, was to invade Zululand ourselves …'[99]

The contemporary opposite view was expressed perhaps most forthrightly by Anthony Trollope:

> Frere, for whom I have both respect and regard, is a man who thinks it is England's duty to carry English civilisation and English Christianity among all the savages. Consequently he has waged war against these unfortunates ... who have lived

side by side us in Natal for 25 years without ever having raised a hand against us!'[100]

In plain terms, Frere was sure that Natal was vulnerable, and in fact, as has recently been argued, the aggressive policy against the Zulus was a consequence of Russian expansionism. He was sure that a Zulu invasion was possible; Chelmsford used the word 'raid' in his memo. Whatever the level of agreement between the two, Trollope's view has held sway in the years since 1879. But the broader view, taking into consideration the Russian context, needs to be examined here, and this possibility has been more exhaustively explored recently by Damian O'Connor. It is necessary to summarize this argument here, because the nature of intelligence in 1879 was very much one in which the politicians and administrators figured in military policy.[101]

The first step is to consider the Forward Policy, which is located for the purposes of Frere and his attitudes to Africa in a particular cabal of three powerful men in the context of the Great Game and Russian threats on the north-west frontier: these were the foremost British authority on the Indian sub-continent, Sir Henry Rawlinson, Henry Bartle Frere himself and Sir Robert Montgomery. In Gladstone's first ministry there had been created the Council of India (1858) as one of the political repercussions of the Mutiny. This was made as a consultative body with ranks of retired administrators from India in it, with the main function of studying, evaluating and formulating important dispatches in the interchange of information between Britain and India. The cabal of three had their main attention on Afghanistan. The head of the Political and Secret Department at the India Office was Sir John Kaye, and he clearly had a good working relationship with the cabal of three elder statesmen. It was Kaye's job to handle state draft replies to secret and political letters from India.

What becomes apparent is that this group of men knew all about the content of secret material that other members of the council would never see. Their exercise of powerful information in the context of the border expeditions in the decades preceding Malakand set a precedent for such involvement in the encroachments into Afghanistan that many wanted. Frere, for instance, had pushed hard for the establishment of a British settlement at Quetta, which is in fact 200 miles over the frontier into tribal lands.

This group first worked together in 1869 and at that time it was a unity founded on the Persian policy. As Britain at the time was reliant for information on a scattered band of agents and spies in a vast area (the one travelled later by Percy Sykes) there was a perception that something more solid and permanent should be put in what was, to all effects, a buffer state which Russia was keen to control. The Forward Policy regarding India by circa 1890 was a natural result of this thinking.

It is stunning to contemplate the machinations of the London-based Political and Secret Department alongside the daily work of intelligence officers and regional political officers, not to mention the work of Montgomerie and the pundits: such a multiplicity of intelligence elements had to work across the vast area of India and bordering states and had to do so in such a way that when something like the Afghan emergency of the retreat from Kabul arose there would be a degree of unity of action and swift communication. The 1842 debacle had a considerable effect on intelligence thinking with regard to the Great Game and to the level of vulnerability trying to cover such a massive area. Africa, too, was vast. At the retreat from Kabul in 1842, forces of the British army and the East India Company were forced to retreat across a vast distance in winter conditions: in a week, over 3,000 soldiers were killed along with 12,000 civilians.

In addition to specific failures and disasters, the Forward group was aware of the front-line reports of officers who had gone behind enemy lines and mixed with the Russians – men such as Frederick Burnaby, whose book *On Horseback through Asia Minor* was published just eighteen months before Chelmsford's column left for Zululand. In Burnaby's book we can sense the growing obsession and paranoia of the Forward thinkers on empire: Burnaby's mission had the central aim of finding out just to what extent Russia had advanced into Turkestan. He cast scorn on the idea expressed by some in Britain that there were benefits in Russia and India being neighbours. He wrote, 'People in this country who advocate the two empires touching are not perhaps aware that our Indian army would then have to be increased to three times its present strength, and in spite of that precaution, there would be less security for ourselves.'[102]

Amazingly, Burnaby planned his journey for winter. His leave of absence from his regiment could only begin in December, and this reminds us that officers engaged in intelligence in the Raj tended to make their contributions in their own time: on official leave for several months, they would often prefer a trek into unknown regions to a trip home. After all, many of them had no family. The way he prepared for the trip, throughout November, is informative on the attitudes behind such intelligence planning. He bought a huge sleeping bag made of sail cloth and took two guns: one for wolves and one (a service revolver) for enemy humans. Essential items such as quinine and cooking materials added to the weight of his burden. But the most intriguing feature of this trip, as in all Great Game journeys, was that liaison with the Russian high command was sought. This was still an era in which officers and gentlemen would converse, be civil and indeed cooperate with actions taken by the enemy. Hence the word *game*. Consequently, Burnaby tried to talk to the Russian War Minister, Milutin, but instead he realized that there had been a breach of etiquette and that Milutin was perturbed:

> I now first learned that General Milutin … was personally opposed to the idea of an English officer travelling in Central Asia, particularly in that part which lies between the boundaries of British India and Russia … a Russian traveller, a Mr Pachino, had not been well treated by the authorities in India. This gentleman had not been permitted to enter Afghanistan and in consequence General Milutin did not see why he should allow an Englishman to do what was denied a Russian subject.

By the 1870s, we have to conclude from this, the Great Game had become a strange concept: on the one hand the military aristocracy still perceived the manoeuvres on both side in attempting to gain intelligence to be a gentlemanly affair, and on the other hand, with pragmatic diplomacy in mind, there was a new Machiavellian ruthlessness emerging. But Burnaby developed a report on military affairs of a practical nature, which he incorporated into his book. For instance, at one point he notes about Kirghiz horses:

> We are apt to think very highly of English horses and deservedly, so far as pace is concerned; but if it came to a question of endurance, I much doubt whether our large and well-fed horses could compete with the little half-starved Kirghiz animals. This is a subject which must be borne in mind in the event of future complications in the East.

More seriously, he assessed the Russian officer class and its attitudes to expansion and open conflict with Britain. The fact was that the officers were often in isolated border areas with little to do but patrol and observe; they could go hunting to enliven their time on duty, but Burnaby saw that there was more than this. He notes,

> You cannot be with Russian officers in Central Asia for half an hour without remarking how they long for a war. It is very natural; and the wonder to my mind is why Russia has not extended herself still farther… and as the only public opinion that is said to exist in the Tsar's empire is represented by the military class, which in a few years will absorb all the male population of the nation, we ought to be thoroughly prepared and ready for an emergency.[103]

Reading Burnaby's book, the reader is staggered by the apparent availability of statistics; he quotes facts and figures that, if accurate, would have been very valuable to all kinds of people, but he himself is not sure of the accuracy and does not give his sources. He writes that if Russian reserves were called out they could put 1.3 million men in the field and that there were 33,893 Turkomen males who could conceivably be one day in active service for Russia. But Burnaby writes that these are 'Russian data' and then admits that there is no way of ascertaining their accuracy. This once again leads us to believe that the agents on the Great Game missions relied on hearsay, chance conversations and any ostensibly 'official' data that might be gained – possibly simply from newspapers.

Writers like Burnaby confirmed the opinions of men in Frere's group that a Forward Policy in the Empire was always going to be, in one way or another, a move against Russia and its aspirations. Damian O'Connor takes all this as a foundation for his examination of Frere's decisions and actions in Zululand. But before looking at O'Connor's argument, some context is needed. As the 1870s went on, Salisbury and his contacts in India and in the Middle East discussed the varying arguments about Russian intentions: was there agreement in Russia that Afghanistan was a target in imperial expansion, or did some Russians believe that more presence in the Middle East was the priority? If the Middle East was indeed a priority, then Frere believed that from there it was an easy task for Russia to have gun boats down to Capetown. A crucially important phase in this attitude to Russia was the period in which the military attaché in Moscow, Sir Frederick Wellesley, became an active spy. From 1872 he had been stealing official papers in Russia. He became spymaster with the Russian War Office as his terrain. He was instrumental in raising other agents to do similar work in other areas, such as in naval intelligence. Salisbury therefore, in the years between 1872 and 1877, knew a great deal about Russian troop movements, correspondence of diplomats and even some letters passing between General Milutin and the Tsar himself.

Disraeli had famously announced that 'Our duty is to maintain the Empire of England' and he was always in favour of supporting Turkey and of settling the issue of the north-west frontier. Espionage was looking increasingly like the best way to do the latter, rather than any ambitious notions about controlling Kabul, although it annoyed Salisbury to think that no 'white man' could negotiate the Khyber Pass with impunity. Ideas about the Russian empire in this decade were apparent largely through the work of Wellesley, a man who had led a chequered career, finding his foothold in St Petersburg because he married the daughter of the British Ambassador there. Earlier he had run off with an actress and blotted his prospects in diplomacy, or so it seemed at the time. But he found his real talents when it came to photographing Russian documents or making enough time for himself to sit and transcribe them.

He also became involved in the risky business of codebreaking. Naturally both Britain and Russia knew that codebreaking was going on, so often the use of misleading and fabricated documents would be encouraged. In 1876 the Russians were becoming more aware of what he might or might not be doing and produced unreliable communications. But Wellesley progressed, and in 1876 he became Military Secretary to the Viceroy. Disraeli himself used Wellesley's materials and information to develop his military attitudes and statements with regard to Russia's imperial intentions.

What the British government really wanted to know was whether or not Russia wanted to take and retain the Middle East. If they did so, then any large force from them in southern Africa would have a supply base closer than any point within the Russian lands. The same applied to work in Afghanistan: hence the journeys to Khiva earlier by the individual officers have their place in the story. But in this period, years after that first phase of the Great Game, general thought began to concur that Russia was more interested in consolidating what she had, notably in Asia Minor – until, of course, Wellesley told Salisbury something different. This happened in 1878, when Wellesley communicated notes on a Russian plan to mobilize and move towards Bokhara.

The problem in London was about how much of Wellesley's reports should be believed and acted upon. Specialist historians on his work and achievement tend to agree that what Wellesley did was to enlighten people in power as to the nature of the Russian mindset when it came to deciding on strategy. What his reports did certainly do was convince the two powerful viceroys, Derby and Lytton, that their attitudes to Russia were right. One of the most influential governors in India at the time of the Mutiny, Lord Lawrence, had represented the older attitudes to Russia – that they would not and could not venture beyond the north-west frontier or from the Middle East. But by the 1870s many were imagining a world in which Cossacks would fight alongside Afghans against the British Army of India, and the mind of Bartle Frere could imagine the horrendous consequences of a Zulu invasion of Natal – if the Russians learned of it.

Damian O'Connor looks at Frere's stance (and also then Chelmsford's as stated in his memo) with these wider Asian and Levantine considerations in mind. He stresses that there was no economic motive in 1879 for the invasion and expansionism in

Africa. He is sure that 'what Britain wanted was control of the route to India, and this meant control of the ports'.[104] In July 1877 Lord Carnarvon escalated fears concerning the ports in southern Africa. At that time it looked very much as though Britain was going to be involved in a war in Europe; Carnarvon insisted that only confederation would settle the African problem, and that consolidation of Britain's position there was paramount. Carnarvon made it clear that the vulnerability of the Cape was something that should be a cause for anxiety, and his friend and fellow Forward Policy thinker, Bartle Frere, backed up the reason for this by writing and talking about the Grand Duke Alexis of Russia visiting the Cape not long before Carnarvon's crusade. Alexis had a gaggle of officers with him, and there had been joking to the British diplomats that they could easily carry off families of politicians and requisition 'a million or two in cash', also 'burning all the coal they did not want for their own ships'.

In November 1877 the Colonial Defence Committee was formed, and it is clear that Carnarvon's deepest desire was that he would be able to do something to protect the Cape. Damian O'Connor argues very powerfully that the origins of the Anglo-Zulu War were in the anxieties about the Cape. Basically, the issue was that if war between Britain and Russia really did happen, what could be done to secure southern Africa if the Tsar turned his attention that way? For a long time, historians and experts on Russian intelligence in the imperial years after the Crimea have noted that such thinking about the Cape was wrong-headed. However, the Russians were certainly investing in espionage: Richard Deacon comments that, 'in the latter part of the last century Russia was easily leading all the great powers in spending on espionage. In 1886 it was calculated that the British and the Germans were spending about £65,000 a year each on their Secret Services, far less than were the Russians …'[105] Russia was also well ahead of Britain in seeing the importance of streamlining military intelligence: as the nineteenth century progressed, more military geography and advanced humint were prominent in the training of officers. From 1864, Russia started to appoint military attachés. There had been a Military Academic Committee since 1815 and so there was a nursery system for the training of spies within the work of military diplomacy. As one historian points out, attachés were crucial to the larger, theoretical workings of intelligence: 'Technically members of embassy staff, enjoying full diplomatic immunity, attaches are intelligence agents, whose main job is to study and report on the armed forces of the host country.'[106] Russia had a corpus of 'main staff' agents, and they would send field agents out on information missions. Now, this was happening in the same way in Britain, but only in the East, from around circa 1830.

There had definitely been an imbalance with regard to the information-gathering taking place with regard to southern Africa as opposed to Africa. In 1875 there were detailed maps pouring from the press on the Middle East and Asia. A company called Stanford, for instance, produced several maps along the lines of 'Stanford's Large-Scale map of the Seat of War in Asia' and Arrowsmith's produced a 'Map of the Acquisitions of Russia in Europe and central Asia since the Accession of Peter I in 1876' (published in 1878).

As O'Connor points out, there was far more to Frere than the apparent war 'fixer' of the Zulu question. He had conceived the main plan of defence for India and had initiated the surveys done by Cunynghame quoted earlier. At the heart of Frere's fears for southern Africa was the fact that if the Balkan War led to the Russians controlling Turkey, then they could soon grasp Suez: if they moved on Cape Town from there, then, as O'Connor puts it, 'the imperial lifelines would be severed with potentially catastrophic results'.[107] Behind this lies the belief among the Forward Policy thinkers that there would be a much more large-scale war with Russia following any defeat in the Balkans. There has always been an entrenched opinion that the Zulu kingdom had no desire to invade southwards; even raids over the Tugela river have always been seen as highly improbable. However, Chelmsford was acutely aware, when he arranged for the dispositions of his columns, that forces were needed at key points because there would be citizens to the south who would be highly vulnerable. That fact alone surely reinforces the view that Frere and Carnarvon had a point. There was no escaping the fact in 1877 that should Russia take Suez and then move on the Cape, there would be inadequate defences to cover such a huge length of coast and such a massive hinterland.

In the Peace Preservation Act of 1878 Frere created a platform for the Cape Mounted Rifles to be reintroduced, something, however limited, that was a measure towards a little more military presence in the defence of the area. Yet that was merely a first step; he wanted imperial armies there. O'Connor defends and explains the reasons why Frere was perceived as he was at the time, and how and why disillusionment set in: 'In reality, Frere reacted to events in places where he could have very little actual day-to-day control. southern Africa is a very big place, and communications were so appallingly bad that he was never able to impose his will ...'[108]

There are few more explicit case studies of military intelligence working from the margins rather than from army decision-making centres than Frere's steps in line with the Forward Policy. He was arguably initiating the kind of policy that needed a system much the same as the military attaché officer, but instead he had a string of colonists, magistrates and political agents. The annexation of the Transvaal and Shepstone's haste to impose unacceptable conditions on Cetshwayo changed matters, of course, and caused a distraction from the kind of realpolitik Frere was trying to impose, as a reaction to what seemed at the time to be the paramount challenge to the Empire – the war in the Balkans and the thought of Russia expanding southwards. Frere had always considered that attack was the best form of defence: he wanted Afghanistan to be the most advanced defence zone in the East, and that had been back in the early 1870s when there were widespread alarmist views on the Russian threat from the north and east in British India. That back-story no doubt has coloured opinions of Frere's later actions in southern Africa.

O'Connor goes on to stress that, after being forced to hold all other matters by the Xhosa revolt in 1877, where Chelmsford was successful, Frere had to work hard to have all armed forces under his control – imperial and colonial. Then there were Zulu raids across their border, and of course we can see in that moment the origins of Frere's later thinking on how and why the Zulu problem had to be understood in terms of a domino effect after the potential Russian advances in the Middle East.

Frere then pressed for the suppression of the Zulus, of course, and again referred to similar moves in India, where there had been successes against native forces. In southern Africa, in the years immediately before the advance into Zululand, comparisons such as that were meaningless; it was a matter of knowing the enemy, and we can see clearly with hindsight that the British and colonial forces did not have the kind of knowledge of the Zulu military mindset that they thought they had. In 1878 intelligence was in the hands of administrators, agents and diplomats, and a perfect example of this is the estimate of Zulu strength by Commodore Sullivan in August 1878, and Governor Bulmer was told to give information about the condition of the Natal artillery. Bulwer and Frere, after gathering information and forming opinions on Zulu strength and capacity, agreed that it could all be summed up with the view that Cetshwayo and his people were a 'perpetual menace'.[109]

At the heart of Frere's military thinking on defence matters was the established fact that the Tugela river could easily be forded at certain times of year. The plain fear of having Zulu *impis* cut a swathe through open, vulnerable country was unbearable. But Frere was considering these matters at the time when Lord Salisbury, the Foreign Secretary, was far more concerned with the Asian Great Game than with other parts of the imperial map. Frere actually wrote to the Queen with his fears, writing that there could be 'a Zulu *impi* in Natal at any one of a hundred places, and would sweep the utterly defenceless country farms and open towns and villages of all life and property'.[110]

O'Connor sums up the actions of Frere in the context of the invasion of Zululand with the rift between Frere and the government at home in mind:

> Frere was only one of a number of colonial administrators who felt justified in waging war against the wishes of London on the grounds that they as 'men on the spot' had a surer grasp of the realities and a better perspective than was available to the politicians a world away in London.[111]

What he did have that was well founded, as intelligence on Zulu intentions, was a number of reports from Shepstone, from Dunn and from Captain McLeod, the political agent in Swaziland, that Cetshwayo had been making diplomatic moves also, and these were thought to be to gain allies in the event of a war.

All this thinking, so clearly and strongly expressed by Damian O'Connor, has certainly opened up debate and offered historians another, less common view of the progress towards war in 1878. One very convincing footnote to Frere's attempts to change military affairs and decisions is the potential German advance in Africa and a possible alliance of their forces with the Boers. That caused yet another dimension to what has later largely been seen as a paranoia on the part of Frere rather than a type of military thinking that actually made sense in terms of why Germany was in Africa – and to a large extent the Berlin Conference of 1884–1885 confirmed Frere's thinking. There, the provisions relating to African possessions were phrased in such a way that future aggressive acts by European powers were defined:

> Any power which henceforth takes possession of a tract of land on the coast of the African continent outside its present possessions … shall accompany that act with a notification thereof, addressed to other signatory powers, to enable them to protest against the same if there exists grounds for them doing so …[112]

Frere's anxiety came from a mix of several possible but not likely events: a Boer rising, a Russian domination of Suez and war in Zululand which had extensions into allies of Cetshwayo elsewhere. That surely explains why few writers and historians before O'Connor have looked at Frere with an open mind. In the study of the Carnarvon push to try to attain a confederation in southern Africa, the factors relating to intelligence have perhaps been overlooked. That has been easy to do, as the various arms of intelligence gathering at the time were rarely synchronized. There is no doubt that Frere had what Clement Goodfellow has called 'a Grand Design' and luckily for future military activity in southern Africa Frere had achieved a great deal in terms of information, if not in terms of an impact on London and on the new regime after the resignation of Carnarvon in January 1878.

As O'Connor has pointed out, the recriminations aimed at Frere after Isandlwana (and of course after the annexation of the Transvaal earlier) defined the way in which he and his reputation have been circumscribed and reduced. It created a tunnel-vision view of the man. O'Connor argues that Frere's situation 'emanated from the fears of a strategic thinker, cut off from most sources of information because of the lack of a telegraph, who did not think that war with Russia could be avoided by negotiation'.[113]

It is not difficult to understand the basis of Frere's anxieties about Russia if we look at publications in 1877–1878 disseminating information about Russia's advances. In *Blackwood's Edinburgh Magazine*, for instance, in July 1878, we have this review of a report on 'New Routes to India': 'Russia had annexed Khiva and Bokhara, and is mustering her battalions on the line of the Oxus ... she has already obtained possession of Kars, Ardahan and Batoum.' It is then added:

> The Russian system of railways is nearly complete as far as Tiflis, and may shortly be expected to reach Reched on the Russo-Persian frontier. It is surmised that this could be extended to the Persian Gulf, which would then be brought into communication with the Black Sea ...[114]

The important point here, with the war of 1879 in mind, is that Frere's thinking and actions were done at a time when military intelligence was operating in southern Africa largely by means other than the new structural placements of attachés and political officers as in India, and with that reliance on low-level humint, as already discussed, based on scouting and on messages conveyed by horsemen. It is the isolation that strikes one now: the fact that southern Africa was then marginal, and that a native war there was always destined to be one of close combat, rapid fire and cavalry advance. In that it was no different from the earlier border wars in India, back in the days of Clive and indeed in the years before circa 1840 when the Russian presence was apparent and growing fast.

For these reasons it is necessary to look at communications and to also link individual stories to the larger picture. If we look at the development of military intelligence in the Victorian period, it is possible to discern these stages: first the gradual emergence of the Intelligence Branch in the military structure of the Empire; then the arrival of influential individuals who played a major role in the professionalization of intelligence; after that the failures of intelligence in prominent campaigns and lessons learned; and finally, the expansion of the integral work of foreign diplomats and attachés who liaised with the newly formed Intelligence Branch of 1873. If we look at the Anglo-Zulu War with this series of phases in mind, we find a pocket of resistance to change – or rather, a separatist status, a place and a military context unlike any other. The reason for this is surely Cetshwayo and the military Zulu nation, who were outstandingly uniquely prepared to defeat the British in those circumstances of 'traditional warfare' in which Britain had assumed superiority after so many encounters so markedly successful.

The Forward school, led by men such as Rawlinson and Frere, may have been defined as deluded and paranoid by later historians, but there is one resolute fact that will not go away: the nations and tribes the imperial armies fought were learning about the British military mindset by the later phase of the Victorian years. They looked and learned, and if they had generals of real merit, they could more than hold their own. There were hundreds of men like Chelmsford who had never realized that.

What we can see in the case of the war of 1879 is that, in terms of the establishment of the Intelligence Branch, the reasons for the real localized intelligence being so piecemeal and pragmatic were that it was largely in the hands of amateurs – knowledgeable ones, of course – but people who were not co-ordinated and briefed in the way that Robertson, working in the Punjab, was, for instance. In addition to that, there were no gazetteers as they were elsewhere: the resulting field intelligence suffered from all this ad hoc work. Ideally, by the late 1870s, fluid and localized intelligence should have been working hand-in-hand. But the sophisticated communications systems were not in place. Hence Frere's anxieties were increased dramatically. This partly explains why this particular war has attracted so much historiography from all quarters: not only was it a traditional conflict with bayonet work and desperate close-up fighting; it was also, as was the case with Custer in the American West, peppered by men of heroic stature, disciplined soldiers who acted without question and trusted in the tested methods of dealing with tribal natives.

The divorce between field intelligence, fluid and unreliable of course at times, and the information-gathering done by diplomats and attachés was marked at this time; intelligence reports before the 1880s were rarely thorough and usually not preserved. In the kind of warfare prevailing in Zululand in 1879, the humint element was crucially important and central to all choices made in command. Attention now turns to the field intelligence undertaken, and to some efforts at improving communication on the battleground.

10

Communications: Humint to Helioscope

Turning attention to the business of spying in traditional warfare, one of the most fruitful ways of understanding what the Zulu spies were up against is to refer to a case study from twenty years after the war in Zululand: the Matabele War of 1896, in which Robert Baden-Powell was head of reconnaissance for Sir Frederick Carrington. The Zulu resources and strategies were, as we have seen, a combination of information-gathering behind enemy lines, diplomatic approaches and field scouting. What is remarkable about Baden-Powell, in spite of some exaggeration later when he became a best-selling author and tended to over-dramatize matters, is that in the Matabele War he did actually act in enemy territory, both behind the lines and in field reconnaissance well in advance of the main forces of the British in the field.

It is easy to dismiss field intelligence work as popular narrative and always rather melodramatic, but we need to recall what was the fate of spies in the African context in the nineteenth century. In the Anglo-Boer War, spies were shot in many cases, almost immediately after interrogation, and Tim Jeal, Baden-Powell's biographer, writes about the fate of some spies in the Matabele War. Admittedly, in this case there had been atrocities against settlers, but still the attitude to spying was adamantly severe:

> In Bulawayo the whites answered these atrocities with mass executions of spies, who were condemned on the flimsiest

> evidence. 'There is a tree,' wrote Frank Sykes, a settler, 'known as the hanging tree to the north of the town, which did service as gallows. Hither the doomed men were conveyed. On the ropes being fastened to their necks, they were made to climb along an overhanging branch, and thence were pushed and compelled to jump into space …'[115]

In 1915, in his book *My Adventures as a Spy*, Baden-Powell wrote about his spycraft in the field and his account of working with his Zulu-born friend Jan Grootboom gives an insight into what could be done, and in fact was clearly normally done, by Zulu spies across their territory as they watched Chelmsford advance. Baden-Powell describes Jan as 'A Zulu by birth, but having lived much with white men, as a hunter and guide, he had taken to wearing ordinary clothes and spoke English perfectly well: but within him he had all the pluck and cunning of his race.'[116] As Baden-Powell and Jan go out to observe the Matabele, very close to the enemy line, Jan's ability to see a trap is evident and he goes on alone. Baden-Powell, aware that even Jan could betray him, hides elsewhere, but then Jan returns and the description perhaps explains perfectly how Cetshwayo's spies knew all the British movements in early 1879:

> He had crept towards them by a devious path, from which he was able to perceive a whole party of the Matabele lying low in the grass by the track by which we should probably have used in getting there, and they would have pounced upon us and captured us … His was an example of a field spy which … demands the greatest personal courage and astuteness.[117]

This is all about that version of intelligence which has always been, since there was warfare involving confrontation in the field, risk and deception. Intelligence about the enemy may of course be utilized by deception of the enemy. When Baden-Powell was holding Mafeking against the Boers, hugely outnumbered, he conducted ruses which simulated the laying of mines and the placement of barbed wire defences. The enemy was fooled. For the Zulu such as Grootboom and the men sent to watch the British columns by Cetshwayo, this was humint in its most basic form. Britain had done this kind of thing – officers in disguise behind enemy lines – across various parts of

Asia and also in the Napoleonic Wars. But once again, against the Zulu there were limitations.

The heart of traditional humint activity has always been low-level technology, pragmatic decisions and calculated risk. It has taken place in the field with almost infinite variations, but it always ultimately involves deviation from established practice and inventive measures of subterfuge and 'invisibility'. Baden-Powell may have become discredited as a reliable source, but the fact is that there is very little else source-wise for the years between circa 1870 and the 1890s. When accounts of autobiographical experience were eventually compiled, or appeared in popular journals in the Edwardian period and the 1920s, the records in official contexts were not available to be used as touchstones of accuracy. Hence the daring exploits of humint intelligence in both field and information-gathering were often written in exaggerated form, mainly because there had been a boom in the publication of male romance after the immense success of H Rider Haggard and others in the 1890s.

The whole area of scouting and study of topography, so important in all military campaigns, is noticeably marginal in the official Intelligence Branch report of 1880, as in this comment on activities in June 1879:

> It had been ascertained that a route suitable for the advance of Wood's column led from Conference Hill to Ibabanango, but as yet no other track had been found by which by which the IInd Division could join in the advance. Hopes were, however, entertained that this long detour might be avoided by the discovery of a more direct line from Landman's Drift …[118]

In other words, the lack of maps was realized, but of course the authors of the official report omitted to say that directly.

Essentially, these limitations were imposed by the nature of communications. Of all the principal aspects of intelligence in war, communication is the one central, inescapable factor in success. Intelligence work sees communications in three main spheres: within the active corps of the army, in the flow of information between staff and the contacts network, and, of course, in the comprehensive sense of mass or large-scale communications. In Zululand, the fundamental fact that there was no telegraph directly between Britain and Cape Town has been much discussed, and forms part of the interpretations of failure so often in the forefront of historians' stances on the war.

The world's first telegraph line was made by Samuel Morse in 1844, running between Baltimore and Washington; his Morse code would later be ciphered, and once again, the 1879 war in southern Africa was too close to the significant advance to have benefited, as the War Office issued *The Manual of Instruction in Army Signalling* in 1876, and it was not until the Boer War of 1899 that interception techniques were used. The most telling statement in that manual is that 'The most accurate way of transmitting intelligence is by means of an orderly carrying a written message.' There had been telegraphs in the form of signal stations in the Napoleonic War, but when the telegraph as such was eventually applied to theatres of war, once again, India benefited. A telegram in the 1857 Indian Mutiny reported 'Cantonment in a state of siege. Mutineers from Meerut … several officers killed and wounded. Troops sent down but nothing yet.' Military leaders in the Punjab saw the massively important value of this. Trevor Fishlock summarized it in this way: 'These messages alerted military commanders, who prudently disarmed their Indian troops to stop the fire spreading. "The electric telegraph has saved us" said a Punjab official.'[119]

By 1865 there was an overhead cable to India and then John Pender arranged a submarine cable, running from Cornwall to Bombay, and that had been finished in 1870. But with regard to southern Africa, it took the Anglo-Zulu War to compel Britain to arrange for a telegraph, but even then, London was not linked to Cape Town until 1887 when the Cape Verde Islands cable was extended. It had taken nineteen days for news of Isandlwana to reach London. As has been noted in the discussion of Bartle Frere, the sense of isolation and the distance from the centre of intelligence policy and strategy were factors in his view of the situation in southern Africa.

In contrast, the heliograph played a considerably important part in the war, notably at Eshowe, to be discussed shortly, but a look at the development of the heliograph is necessary first. In classical times, a shield well polished was some kind of basic heliography, but the first recorded use of a heliograph (technically a heliotrope) was in 1821 as a method of utilizing beams of sunlight. The heliostat had a mirror that did not oscillate, and that was being used in the work of the Indian Army in 1869, developed by Sir Henry Mance.

The heliograph had several advantages: it was light and easily carried, it needed no power source other than sun, and in southern Africa there was sunlight in abundance, and it was not traceable if it was positioned well away from the recipient. It was basically two mirrors on a stand with a lever arm and a beat regulating screw, using a jointed sighting rod and a linked sighting vane. The clearest account of its use comes from R F Naylor, historian of the Royal Corps of Signals:

> In essence it comprised two mirrors fixed at right angles to each other, one being silvered and the other unsilvered. The operator looked through the unsilvered mirror at the distant station and turned the pair of mirrors so as to superimpose the relatively faint image of the sun reflected from the plain surface of the of the unsilvered mirror onto the distant station. This automatically directed the beam reflected from the plain mirror onto the distant station ...'[120]

The heliograph was also the subject of study and development by scientists as well. In fact, amazingly, once again the Russian connection rears its head, because scientists in Britain had been making heliographs for the Russian government just a few years before the war in southern Africa. Writing in 1872, Professor de la Rue of the Royal Society wrote to Professor Stokes about this work, just a year after receiving a £200 fee from Russia. He said,

> I have been able to introduce many improvements both in the mechanical parts and in the optical portion of the instrument but I did not think it desirable to interrupt the sun-work to make any changes in the Kew heliograph. Now that the work is completed I would recommend that the secondary magnifier should be changed to the form adapted in the instrument made for the Russian government under my direction ...[121]

We can see from this that British expertise was well advanced in astronomical uses as well in military, but also that Russia was prepared to pay for that expertise. No doubt de la Rue never thought about the military benefits for the Tsar.

It was in India that the heliograph was being used widely and effectively in the field. In some regimental workshops in 1877, Lieutenant G R R Savage, Inspector of Signalling at Roorkee, was working with Sergeant Martin and some sepoy craftsmen on a heliograph, and then in the Second Afghan War of 1878–1880 there were sappers and miners who were defined as telegraph units. There was also a heliograph detachment in the Khyber Pass at that time.

In the battle of Ahmed Khel in 1880 a field telegraph was used and there was a heliograph battery used in the communications between Peshawar and Kabul. It was recorded that a range of fifty-six miles had been achieved there. Even more significant for future uses in intelligence, as Major Harfield wrote:

> After the battle of Ahmedkel [sic] it was considered vital to communicate with the column under the command of Sir John Ross. A reconnaissance was sent from Ghazmi to the Sher-i-Daton Pass and in the absence of cavalry signallers three officers accompanied the heliograph. On reaching the pass the heliographs were set up and within a few minutes both the advance and the rearguard of Sir John Ross's column were picked up at a distance of about 30 miles and lists of those killed and wounded at Ahmedkel were transmitted.[122]

There is yet another deep irony in this development of the device in India. As officers in Zululand were toying with the idea and working by trial and error at Eshowe, in India it was so popular that its use had to be controlled. Not only army staff but also journalists began to want to use it and to send longer and longer messages. Signals were then limited to a hundred words and each person could send only one message each day, and the messages all had to be approved. But use became sophisticated and effective, and by the 1880s there were records from the Central Signalling School at Kasauli recording messages sent over distances of eighty-three miles from a twelve-inch type heliograph.

By the side of this, the events on the Tugela river, in which Lieutenant Haynes managed to send signals to Fort Eshowe, were moderate. The story of that success, in which eventually Major Wynne, fatally ill and using toilet mirrors initially, established contact is one of the intelligence triumphs of the Anglo-Zulu War. The fullest account of this has been written by Lieutenant Colonel David Mullineaux and my account owes a great deal to his research. Naturally, the use of the heliograph at Eshowe was featured in the 1880 official intelligence report, but only briefly. The main point here is that the instruments used at the Tugela and Eshowe were not technically heliographs, but arrangements of mirrors and other materials that would offer the same communicative functions. Mullineaux, whose article is through and painstakingly analytical, has clarified this: 'It has to be concluded that there were no heliograph instruments, and that, even allowing for artistic licence, [Melton] Prior's sketch is historically inaccurate and misleading – just a product of his imagination perhaps – based on a written description based on a "heliograph"...'[123] Mullineaux also clarifies the vocabulary which has to be used here:

> The distinction between telegraphy and signalling should perhaps be explained ... It was contemporary usage for 'telegraphy' to refer to the *electric* telegraph and 'signalling' to refer to visual signalling, even though the purist would be correct in saying that telegraphy, literally 'writing at a distance', applies to both ...'[124]

Mullineaux's analysis of the whole story of the mirror signalling between Eshowe and the St Andrew's station near the Tugela provides a fascinating account of the ingenuity and enterprise of Royal Engineers officers, in complete contrast to their Indian counterparts with their manuals and special training. In fact, it is arguably one of the very best examples of field intelligence as traditional reconnaissance would have conceived it – all about ad hoc trial and error methods and teamwork. The men involved come across as stunningly inventive: a credit to the Royal Engineers' training at Woolwich, where a wide spectrum of skills and field preparations were provided. It was almost a cultivated mindset in that regiment to prepare for the unexpected, hence the success of the defence strategies at Rorke's Drift, of course. There are countless case studies of similar response to urgent requirements in the field across the tract of imperial history, but few can match this for sheer dogged determination and a 'Heath Robinson' approach that eventually won the day, though Chelmsford and others had initially scoffed at the idea of signalling with the sun's rays to the beleaguered garrison at Eshowe.

The story concerns the period of the siege of Eshowe for almost two months early in 1879, after Colonel Charles Pearson had advanced across the Tugela. He had heard of Isandlwana and decided not to retreat but to dig in. He was, of course, surrounded by Zulus and matters were looking very bleak. Fort Pearson was over twenty miles south of Eshowe on the lower Tugela drift, and close to the fort, at St Andrews, where the signalling had taken place initially, in the hands of Lieutenant Haynes. Eshowe was also considerably higher than Fort Pearson.

With Pearson was Captain Warren Wynne, who had come out to work on fortifications along with Haynes as the Royal Engineers were destined to move inland towards Eshowe. But it was decided that Wynne would move forward while Haynes, with a small detachment, would stay at Durban. Later, Haynes followed, but then Wynne, with Pearson, was trapped and surrounded. Haynes was with Chelmsford and the gradually reconstituted forces when the problem of communicating with Pearson became paramount. It was Haynes who first thought of a heliograph of some kind. The first source for what he did comes from a journalist on the *Western Morning News*, who wrote that Chelmsford and his staff were 'far from sanguine' but that inventiveness and necessity took over and Haynes used a bedroom looking glass at first. It took a while, as the journalist noted, and 'long after a less persevering man would have given up the trial an answering gleam was seen from the Eshowe church tower'.[125] Haynes had used a mirror apparently taken from a hotel, and there had been a small measure of success. Mullineaux notes that Wynne recorded events and he wrote that by 4 March signalling was quite satisfactory and 'we were able to reply by means of a looking glass'.[126]

In Chelmsford's dispatch in March there was confirmation of a communication with Eshowe, and a native runner had managed to get through and report that the signalling was effective. Chelmsford wrote that this had been done simply by 'flashing signals'. The problem then was whether Wynne at Eshowe could reply, and his story is one of hugely impressive resolve and dedication to the task. The Royal Engineers at that time were responsible for almost every conceivable kind of communication and survey, and Wynne was quite accustomed to the need to use trial and error. His diary notes:

> March 3rd Today the signalling from the Tugela was observed and some words. This of course caused much excitement. I determined to try and effect communication by means of a large screen raised above the ground, revolving on horizontal pivots, which, being brought alternately to a horizontal and vertical position in front of the places to be signalled to, should produce dashes and dots through the spaces of time of its appearance.[127]

This did not work, but his second attempt was fine and he noted that they sent some signals over a period of a few hours. He was using a kind of shutter telegraph, basic and unsatisfactory, but at least there was some level of communication. Wynne was still thinking hard on this when he became seriously ill with fever, and he died on 9 April.

Captain Henry Grey MacGregor took over the responsibility for the signalling and he described the challenge of perfecting the messages: he noted that the flashes produced were inadequate and that cloudy weather was frustrating them still further. Amazingly, it was when a bedroom mirror was found and this replaced the small shaving mirror they had previously tried to use that the flashes became adequate. The issue here was that as the relation of Eshowe to Fort Pearson is close to a direct north–south line, the sun was to the north, and so for Haynes at St Andrews it was a plain matter of taking the sun directly and reflecting it back northwards, whereas for MacGregor the sun was behind the mirror. The other problem was that a true heliograph needs a second mirror, a duplex, so that the recipient has the light from the fixed duplex. What was created at

Eshowe was a heliostat – two mirrors at right angles, taking the sunlight directly to the recipient.

MacGregor had his device made essentially as a heliostat. Later, in a lecture in 1880, MacGregor explained what he had done at Eshowe. 'At each end of a long straight tube a piece of paper was fixed. The tube was then aligned on the distant flash. Next the mirror was set up so that both pieces of paper were lit by the sun's reflection, and by this means we knew that the flash was visible from the distant station.'[128] But as Lt Col Mullineaux has researched, there is another version, written by Lieutenant Thomas Ryder Main of the 2nd Field Company, Royal Engineers. He assigns success to Colonel Forestier-Walker of the Scots Guards, who mounted a mirror so that it was fixed on a barrel but mobile horizontally. Ryder wrote: 'So we turned down and eventually solved the mystery in a very simple manner by two directing rods of thin iron with pens on the top. This arrangement was not perfect but we were at last in contact with the outer world …'[129] There are even conflicting testimonies in other sources as to who was right here – MacGregor or Main. But as Lieutenant Colonel Mullineaux showed in the *Illustrated London News* (whose Melton Prior was taking a special interest in the activities of the Engineers) there were drawings of both methods.

There is also the evidence of the Signalling Station message book from St Andrews, and this has a sketch showing what was done there: shadow spots were created so that the angle of the mirror could be adjusted. There was a high degree of success at last, and of course it became much in demand for family communications as well as official ones. By late March this had been supervised and the signalling was used for information reports.

Lieutenant Colonel Mullineaux has closely examined a variety of visual and written sources on the use of heliographs generally throughout the war, and he has highlighted all the distortions and errors on the contemporary press. However, these myriad articles demonstrate the widespread and intense interest in the heliograph in the general and scientific press in Britain in the years immediately after 1879, and H Baden Pritchard, writing in 1880, pointed out the main virtues:

> On the other hand, sunshine signals have material advantages that must not be overlooked. The cost of working over a distance of twenty to fifty miles is much less with mirrors than with the electric telegraph, even supposing oxy-hydrogen lamps were provided for night-signalling. Again, an enemy cannot read your signals, because he has no guide to direct him, neither is it possible for him to cut off your communications, so readily done in the case of the electric telegraph, by severing the wire.[130]

There were plenty of other technical developments with reference to field intelligence, of course. Ballooning, for instance, had been used for military purposes since the Battle of Fleuris in 1794 and observation balloons were used at the siege of Mainz. Ballooning had had a very shaky and intermittent start in Britain; in 1837 a balloonist called Cocking flew above Vauxhall in a balloon with a parachute attached and the experiment cost him his life. There had been ballooning since the first achievements of the Montgolfier brothers in the late 1700s, but in Britain it was Henry Coxwell who suggested military uses. The army responded and a manual was written on the subject by Lieutenant Turner, who wrote that Coxwell in 1854 had demonstrated successful flying in this way. Coxwell added semaphore arms to his balloon, and Coxwell insisted that he had the main advantage over the heliograph that the sun was not required, of course. *The Illustrated London News* produced some engravings in 1879, linking this to signalling in general, and noted that 'Mr Coxwell states that that they would be applicable to hot air balloons as well as to gas, and he suggests a due provision of each kind for signal purposes, as well as for a mean of escape …' and that 'In our engraving the balloon is being let up by windlass machinery such as might be improvised near a fortress or in the field and the military aeronaut is signalling intelligence.'[131] In August 1879 a Military Balloon Committee was developing this, and what they tried was again reported: 'By means of a newly-contrived double furnace they have succeeded in producing hydrogen gas much more rapidly than heretofore, and of very superior buoyancy … Captain Elsdale of the Royal Engineers, one of the committee, on Saturday ascended alone in the Saracen.'[132] He was successful in flying to Rye but could not descend without the help of people on the ground, who had to grasp ropes which he threw down, otherwise he would have been going across the Channel. In 1879, all this was distinctly at the experimental stage. There were plans then to try other materials for the balloon, including goldbeaters' skin. The search was on for something that was guaranteed to be gas-tight.

Again, as so often noted here, the year of 1879 was just on the cusp of the trajectory of British military development, because it was in 1878 that a Balloon Equipment Store was established at Woolwich and the main problem – that of having to make hydrogen in the field with portable equipment – had been solved, as had the issue of having a suitable material for battle applications. But it was in 1885, in the Bechuanaland, that balloons were used by British forces; they were used later in the Anglo-Boer War also. Kitchener as a young man went to join the French forces in 1870, and there he took part in balloon operations.

At the same time, the telephone was just emerging as a facility. As a writer called George Dodd wrote in 1879: 'Military men are studying the problem of applying this instrument to the strategy and tactics of war. The autumn maneouvres, in both France and Germany, of 1878, have been marked by the use of the telephone for outpost work …'[133]

The same applies to photography. In 1868 there had been Royal Engineers photographers and in southern Africa there were some Royal Engineers personnel taking photographs, though most images were taken by civilians. Royal Engineers photographers took pictures at Isandlwana, Rorke's Drift and Eshowe; there were also photos taken by officers of 5 Company, and by men of Wood's Irregulars, notably George Ferneyhough.[134] In intelligence terms, the Natal photographers, men who provided the best record of people and events, had incidentally made a useful resource for future staff and theorists looking at the war – as a learning experience. It was in the 1870s that the technology arrived enabling a dry plate with salts in gelatine to provide instant use, preserving the negative to be developed later. It was not until the 1890s that photography was applied fully and its use in intelligence accepted.

This survey has highlighted the nature of the technology behind the basic messenger and runner communications in warfare of this kind. The conclusion has to be that the Anglo-Zulu War was placed fatefully at a dark spot, an eclipse as it were, of the development of field intelligence technology. Only a few years after Wolseley was established, following Chelmsford, things were to begin to change. The centre of operations in London, concerned from 1876 with information-gathering above all, was slowly to realize the virtues of investing in the modern, mechanized elements of intelligence work. But there was no real advance until Kitchener, largely through the use of the railway, was victorious at Omdurman against the Mahdi. By then (1898) there were signs of an army that was to be streamlined in terms of rigid, operational rationalization – but even that was only on the surface. There would always be humint, and staff risking their lives scouting and observing in dangerous locations.

Historians of military intelligence inevitably look at the wider context of warfare and states in the 1870s, and comparison of Britain with Prussia, for instance, in a case study of field ciphers is a classic template for showing the shortcomings of British intelligence. The Director of Prussian Intelligence, Wilhelm Stieber, had established the Abwehr in the 1840s, with spies using ciphers, such as 'Agent 17', who was operating in Paris. This was August Schluga, and he was working with the German military attaché there, a certain Alfred von Waldersee. The ciphers used had been developed by the Prussians, and after codes being used in the diplomatic sphere, efforts were made to develop a field cipher. In 1883 Auguste Kerckhoffs' *La Cryptographie Militaire* was published, and that made apparent the progress made by Prussia in this respect. In other words, this was not really happening in Britain, particularly as Lord Palmerston had erased the long-standing Secret Office in 1847 – a small but talented cadre who intercepted mail and who were the kinds of minds to be applied in codemaking and codebreaking.

11

Theorists, Amateurs and Soldiers

Moving now to the immediate responses and the reflections and intelligence opinions in the decades after the Anglo-Zulu War, it is useful and enlightening to see what the war against the Zulus taught the Victorians and how the later development of the Intelligence Branch, as well as discussions in popular culture, utilized the sheer pragmatic successes of the Zulu campaigns. In many ways, the years between Ulundi and the outbreak of the Anglo-Boer War of 1899 was a time when ideas and debates on military intelligence were a mix of amateur and academic. But at the heart of the continued references to the Zulu military machine there was respect and admiration such as no other native army had received. Perhaps the ultimate example of this is a letter to *The Daily Graphic* in 1890:

> Sir, In your issue of Saturday last you had an article on the employment of native troops in our tropical colonies and dependencies, and referred to an enquiry which is being made by the Imperial Government on the expediency of raising such a force in Zululand from among the Zulu people. It may perhaps interest some of your readers to know that this idea is anything but new, and that offers have been made to the military authorities at the War Office … There is no doubt that the Zulus would make first-class soldiers, and I do not think anything would raise the morale of the nation more than by

> making them feel … that the Great Queen had asked them to become part of her army.[135]

If we leave aside the sickening sense of superiority here, the fact is apparent that, as in the long tradition of empires assimilating the best in their conquered peoples reaching back to Rome, this is a massive compliment to the Zulu fighter. But the really important point here is what this letter represents. After the 1870s and that decade's massive conflicts in India and Africa, and the almost unthinkable war against Russia that never happened, there was a widespread and vibrant interest in military matters, and notably in intelligence.

THEORISTS

Spenser Wilkinson is perhaps a representative figure here. In an essay in a journal in 1899 he wrote 'On the Art of Going to War', and he says there, 'The French government in 1870 forgot to ascertain in time the strength of the German army, and by going to war with a light heart foredoomed its whole regular army to defeat and capture.'[136]

Wilkinson was one of many military writers who made military failure exciting, interesting and significant. He taught military history and wrote widely in popular periodicals about imperial wars and other European conflicts. Wilkinson's account of how he coped with the dangerous situation of being arrested as a spy in Cracow is a paradigm of the mental combat required in such diplomatically tough situations. He played every card he could think of, including the 'fellow officers and gentlemen' one; he also spoke coolly about his role as a war correspondent and then about his deep sympathies with Austria. None of this had much effect and he was asked to produce his papers. The Commissary was a hard man. It was when his property was searched that Wilkinson must have feared the worst: 'Now began an examination of papers from my bag; and to tell the truth my heart sank within me as the Commissary took up a handful of greetings cards.' There were two cards from high-ranking Prussian officers. He had even bought some maps of Cracow. Even the most youthful tyro in the ranks of the police would not have failed to see Wilkinson as a guilty man. He was taken to a citadel to make written depositions. He must have felt the shadow of a firing squad over him at that moment.

The situation grew more ominous when a clerk changed his statement to make the words read as assertions that here was a spy. Luckily, Wilkinson had fluent German and he worked hard to have that put right. His original words were written down in the nick of time. The occasion became one of a battle of wills and intellects between the prisoner and the Commissary. After a night in a cell, Wilkinson was told he could walk free for some hours if he swore to return to the office that afternoon. This was the turning point of the spying adventure and it took sheer brainwork to extricate the man from his captivity:

> I replied, I think not. You publicly arrested me last night as a spy. All the Cracow papers this morning will announce that you have caught a spy. Now you want to turn me out on the mob. That does not suit me. You will have to take care of me yourselves until you have quite done with me ...[137]

The conclusion of the tense arrest and inquisition was that his cultural acquisitions and fluency with both languages and thought extricated Wilkinson. His account of dining with the Governor and Commissary reads like an episode from a James Bond film. He had stayed calm, and, as the Governor admitted, the general view had been that Wilkinson was a Russian spy, as the Cracow authorities had captured several such men. He had been followed and observed all day and they had expected him to fight his way out, as they realized he was British. His calmness and frankness had won the day. Not only did he go free and continue his journey to Vienna, but he asked his captors if there was anything about their preparations for war in Cracow that they did not wish to be printed.

The Wilkinson adventure illustrates that element in espionage at the time that might be called the 'dockyard visit' experience. Notable people, from royalty down to top industrialists and financiers, could make official visits to dockyards, take notes, ask questions and return home with details of ships, guns, tonnage and so on. This was the same strange openness that Younghusband had found when Russian officers in Manchuria had asked him to tea and given him some military statistics. Readers were taking an increasingly keen interest in both field intelligence and diplomatic information-gathering. The Zulu War presented a fertile field of enquiry and discussion for these new interests. Looking at this debate offers a chance to understand what Isandlwana and Rorke's Drift in particular meant – how they cast a long shadow over both popular culture and military history.

LATER RESPONSES

The accounts of the war at the end of 1879 and throughout the following year confirm the opinion that the contrast between Chelmsford and Wolseley was the common way of understanding what intelligence work had been applied. A number of writers took the view, as expressed by John Crowdy referring to 1879 for instance, that

> Sir Garnet Wolseley took with him to Natal at least one idea: it was to repeat in Zululand the measure by which he had enabled his soldiers to advance and conquer in the Ashanti country, the employment, namely, of natives to fetch and carry while the Europeans led the fighting. But Sir Garnet had no occasion to test the efficacy of his plan ...[138]

Generally, Wolseley was credited with the success in taking Cetshwayo, as Alan Bott noted, writing in 1900: 'Wolseley, arriving after Ulundi, directed the rounding up and capture of Cetshwayo, completed the Zulu subjugation and came home in 1880.'[139] Long after his time in the war, Archibald Forbes was still insisting on comparing Wolseley and Chelmsford, and he was profoundly influential on how later writers saw the control and direction of intelligence in 1879. Writing a profile on Wolseley in 1899, Forbes reported on an interview with the great general, and the latter explained how his intelligence officers were selected, thinking no doubt of Brackenbury and Maurice:

> I know these men of mine [he says in effect], and they know me. I selected them originally because of my discernment of character, not at the behest of interest or from the dictates of

> nepotism. We have worked long together; their familiarity with my methods and my just reliance on them, relieves me of half the burden of command.[140]

On the other hand, as time had passed, Chelmsford's decisions on tactics gathered complimentary comments, such as, in 1900, Charles Stein's account of Ulundi and Hlobane, which includes positive statements on Chelmsford's 'watchfulness' and also on the 'strenuous exertion' he showed in gathering a force on the river strong enough to march on Eshowe.[141] Chelmsford's actions after Gingindlovu and Eshowe certainly turned the tide of opinion after the initial period of criticism, and even in 1880 there were assessments that understood how he redeemed himself to a large degree in his efforts to improve communications and to have knowledge of the enemy more consistently to hand, but even then the compliments were back-handed. One writer noted that he was 'a gentleman worthy of respect with a readiness which indicated the opinion that he was little more and certainly not a military genius'.[142]

Naturally there were more fundamental factual matters to be appraised: the subject of maps and cartography was one. After the Anglo-Boer War of 1899–1902 there was an inquisition on the maps available and their use, as once again it was seen that this insufficiency had been a factor in the failure. Similarly, the maps used in Zululand are a puzzling topic. Melton Prior has a drawing of officers studying a map of the country, published in the *Illustrated London News*, and we have to wonder what that might have been. As previously mentioned, there were maps of the Transvaal of course, and the border agents and interpreters, missionaries and magistrates provided some. But as noted earlier, Henry Curling made the point that there was a lack of accurate maps, and he writes that the Royal Engineers 'took the opportunity to survey and produce the first accurate maps of the region'. How did they do this? Prior has drawings of engineers using balloons with signalling attachments, and by implication that device must have been used at times for some surveying, but the area is vast: 10,450 square miles.

It has to be surmised that the mapping going on was piecemeal, partial and intermittent. In 1880, as discussed in chapter 9, maps of southern Africa generally were being produced commercially, but nothing on the scale of what William Robertson was doing at the Intelligence Branch. Robertson wrote in his memoirs of his time in the Intelligence Branch working on information regarding topography and human geography: 'The Intelligence Branch was responsible for the collection and collation of military information regarding foreign countries, but it was not the recognised duty of the branch … scientifically to study the information and make it the basis of our own requirements.' But even twenty years after Ulundi, as Robertson notes, as he was working in southern Africa, 'I had to rely for my data largely upon the reports of war correspondents, which would often appear in the press before the same information reached me officially, and sometimes the newspapers alone supplied the particular intelligence I wanted.'[143]

When it came to cartography, again southern Africa was well behind India. From the 1840s there had been a steady survey, using native pundits, with agents walking for vast distances monitoring the land and the roads. But as Robertson says, when it came to collecting and filing information on foreign states where wars were likely, or which worked as buffer states between warlike nations or tribes, there was still a large amateurish element in intelligence work around 1890. Robertson notes that 'There were in the Foreign Section some small non-confidential handbooks largely compiled from newspapers and other unofficial publications, which related to the strength and organisation of most of the foreign armies. These … did not contain anything of much value in regard to strategical questions ...'[144] The closest equivalent to a dossier on Zulu military capability would possibly be the information from John Dunn.

There were geographers who had paid some attention to Zululand, notably Keith Johnston, but again, his work was not completed until after 1879. In 1891 he published his *Half-Crown Historical Atlas*, and this included maps of the Zulu and Boer conflicts of 1879–1880, the Ashanti War of 1873–1874 and the Egyptian map at the time of the war in the 1880s. Johnston was working in Natal at the time of the war and his activities in taking the first steps towards good maps were reported. We have to ask which maps the officers in Prior's illustration of officers reading a map in Zululand were using.

Possibly they were draft versions of Johnston's but it is almost certain that there were maps of small areas, parts of the theatre of war that had been scouted and then sketched in situ.

From 1853 the Royal Military Corps had begun to produce a standard map scale. From that time there was a steady but desultory sequence of projects undertaken to survey and map the various pink areas of the great map of Empire. Kitchener, for instance, was given the task of surveying Cyprus, after doing the same for Palestine. He wrote, on beginning the task in 1878, to Cobbold, the MP who had given him the job: 'Thank you for a most delightful appointment … It is exactly what I like and will be a great advancement for me professionally when I have done it. I expect I shall take two and a half to three years to finish it.'[145] We have to wonder at the lack of system behind the cartography, undertaken not by the Intelligence Branch, of course, but done ad hoc. When Kitchener began surveying Palestine the Arabs thought he was working on a Christian plot to take the land, and there was a serious confrontation in 1875 when the surveyors were attacked by an armed gang.

There was a definite reason why Cyprus had been chosen for Kitchener to map and survey: it was only 200 miles from the Suez Canal and was just 100 miles from Alexandretta, the planned terminus of the Euphrates Valley Railway. Frere would have approved of that particular map-making venture. It was widely thought in 1879 that as Russia had taken Kars she may try to carry out what were often called 'designs' – whatever they might have been.

In 1873 Wolseley was in charge of the Intelligence Branch and took a close interest in the work done in relation to intelligence work at the Staff College. In 1879, after six years of establishment, there were nine officers at Sandhurst teaching military survey; at the Staff College there was one lecturer in drawing and surveying, one teaching military history and one teaching Hindustani. The Royal Engineers' training at Woolwich still had the monopoly on the practical and technical elements of intelligence for field and reconnaissance. Robertson makes it clear that his acquirement of military intelligence knowledge at the Staff College was linked to theoretical and tactical studies, led by Henderson, a man destined to be one of the principal officers for intelligence against the Boers. Woolwich included landscape drawing, military drawing and military history. Since the 1830s, however, at Woolwich, direct education regarding intelligence work was marginal. As Anthony Clayton has said in his assessment of army training in the first three decades of the nineteenth century: 'little need was seen for any staff training in subjects such as organisation, movements, language or intelligence'.[146] So these were introduced by the 1850s really, when lessons learned in the Crimea changed everything.

It is significant that, inheriting Thomas Best Jervis's establishment of cartography as a central rung in the military intelligence ladder in the 1850s, the new Intelligence Branch appeared to be still working and training separately from the Royal Engineers, whose business had always been cartography and surveying. The Cardwell Reforms of 1871 (the Regulation of the Forces Act) had created a combined department in which three executive officers operated: one of these was the Surveyor General of the Ordnance. Essentially, this meant that the Royal Engineers would still have the central responsibility for cartography, though Jervis's claims for it as central to intelligence work had receded. The unfortunate consequences of this narrow-sightedness may be seen in the debate over the maps in 1902 when Sir John Ardagh was taking severe criticisms as head of the Intelligence Branch.

One of Ardagh's more interesting achievements came about in a way that illustrates the spy's best friend – sheer serendipity. But the story also illustrates the mess in the army with regard to how cartography should have been valued. We know this tale of the acquisition of Transvaal maps because an account was written by the famous military historian Brigadier General J E Edmonds in 1922. His account was from the standpoint of a man who was actually Ardagh's agent in this minor triumph. His story was that in December 1899 the British minister in Berne, Sir Francis St John, noticed a large-scale map on a wall in an antechamber of the federal building there. It was a map of the Transvaal and the creator of this very useful item was an inhabitant of Zurich, so the diplomat noted the name, then contacted him. Sir Henry Angst, a senior diplomat, saw to it that knowledge was gained about other copies of the maps.

It was discovered that three thousand of them could be bought for £3,000. Edmonds then completes the saga in *The Times:*

> Sir Francis St John communicated with London and a high officer of the Foreign Office brought his telegram to the old Intelligence Offices at 18, Queen Anne's Gate. Sir John Ardagh instructed me to go to the War Office in Pall Mall, see the permanent Under-Secretary, Sir Ralph Knox, and stay there until I got the authority for the money.

Edmonds obtained what he wanted and travelled to Berne immediately. He was taken by Angst to Winterthur where the maps were all packed and ready for movement. He notes that 'The production of the proof-sheet settled the matter. I took as many maps as I could carry back with me, arriving in England on Christmas Eve. Mr Angst dispatched the cases of maps to my private address, where they arrived safely.' In other words, although one case of maps had been sent to southern Africa already before all this took place, the fact was that the map was found by chance and Ardagh only obtained copies because of a chance sighting by a man walking through a room, doing other business.

Up to the 1890s, it is noticeable that investment in intelligence work from the branch was still focused on India. The Afghan Frontier Commission of 1885 was featured in *The Times* and it was reported that the intelligence staff were extending survey work. Sir Peter Lumsden wrote in his report:

> Captain P J Maitland, Bombay Staff Corps and Captain W Peacocke, R.E., Deputy Assistant Quartermasters-General of the Indian Intelligence Branch, were most energetic in collecting and collating a vast amount of information as to the country and people and also in assisting the Survey Department, with whom they worked with the greatest cordiality.[147]

In fact, intelligence work in the East was becoming more commercial than ever. Lists of new books published in the 1880s often included accounts of work being done in the buffer states, such as *From Korti to Khartoum*, which was a journal of a desert march from Korti to

Gubat 'and of the ascent of the Nile in General Gordon's steamers' by Colonel Sir Charles Wilson. He was Deputy Adjutant of the General Intelligence Branch.

UNDERSTANDING THE ZULU SUCCESS

In the history of British military intelligence, the results of the defeat at Isandlwana, and indeed the many other embarrassing events such as the death of the Prince Imperial, were that commentators, both military and civilian, were made to think again about 'tribal' enemies. Naturally there had been Kabul in 1842 and other earlier disasters, but 1879 in southern Africa had shown that it might be a good idea in future to know something about native armies – and of course native peoples generally, their culture and beliefs. One of the most cogent responses in this respect was from the *Westminster Review* in April 1879:

> The terrible disaster in Zululand which has lately befallen our usually victorious troops has roused the whole nation to desire to know more of a people and a country perhaps hitherto too slightly regarded. We are so apt to consider a war with barbarous tribes on the frontiers of our remote colonies as a matter of small moment, and to look upon victory as certain, that the news of the massacre of eight hundred of our gallant troops … by a horde of naked savages took everyone by surprise ...[148]

These perceptions changed and the words 'naked savages' were to be reversed and questioned – hence the suggestion that Zulu warriors would make a sepoy regiment. There followed, throughout the early 1880s, a continuing interest in Zulu matters, and they were recognized as having an 'army' rather than a 'horde' as the respect grew, and in fact they became distinctly separate in the public mind from other tribal foes. As writing on them increased so did the more incisive and profound accounts of their military system and achievements. The only problem was that this was always seen as expansionist, because the 'washing of the spears' had been a phrase that had stuck in the mind of the general public. In 1880, for example, one writer commented:

> In the words of Sir Bartle Frere, the Governor of the Cape, to whom the Zulu War is undoubtedly due, the Zulu army was a 'celibate man-slaying machine' … The really distinctive feature of the Zulu army, and that which made the Zulu power an intolerable neighbour, was that it existed for the sake of killing …'[149]

The impression made by the Zulu army and the courage in the field, assegais against guns, made a considerable impression in literature also. Apart from H Rider Haggard's string of novels featuring Zulu characters, there were poems such as 'Brave Beresford' by H D Rawnsley, in which we have:

> But we saw on a sudden the mighty Zulu,
> With the ring on his head and the shield on his arm,
> Up-gather himself for the deed he would do …[150]

In later discussions on Isandlwana other aspects of Zulu actions came out. In August 1880, for instance, Lieutenant Colonel Edward Durnford responded to Lord Ellenborough's account of the battle, blaming Colonel Durnford for the disaster. J L A Simmons defended Durnford and then Edward added:

> Lord Chelmsford knew before he left the camp that the enemy was in the neighbourhood [not the main Zulu army] and the responsibility as to precautionary measures was with him. Could Col. Durnford know of the 20,000 Zulus lying *perdus* some five miles off? How came they there unknown?[151]

Durnford had taken command at the camp at around ten o'clock in the morning and he heard the threat coming nearby; he had no reason to think that the main Zulu army was there. Chelmsford had said that Durnford had stated that he was going to go out and prevent the First Column from joining the force supposed to be at that time engaged with the troops with Chelmsford.

The debates of 1880, after the anniversary of Isandlwana, opened up these kinds of reappraisals, and so the Zulu military culture was slowly understood and written about. In September of that year a book by Captain H H Parr, *Guadana to Isandlwana: A Sketch of the Zulu and Kaffir War*, was published. Parr had been on the personal staff of Frere and so his interpretation was sure to be coloured by the Confederationist views. His most influential views were those blaming Cetshwayo, and his account of the King's intrigues and diplomacy presents a ruler as subtle and articulate in theoretical intelligence as the top officers in the British army. If Parr is to be believed, Cetshwayo was at the centre of all dissension in the year before the war began. He wrote: 'Wherever magistrates reported uneasiness or discontent among the natives, wherever a native rising took place, there was Cetshwayo's influence at work.'[152]

The novelist H Rider Haggard did more than most to popularize and instruct the general reader on the real nature of the Zulu military state. His novel on Shaka, *Nada the Lily*, for instance, sets out partly to show its military organization: 'The Zulu military organisation, perhaps the most wonderful in its way that the world has seen, is already a thing of the past; it perished at Ulundi. It was Chaka [sic] who invented that organisation, building it up from small beginnings.'[153] With this kind of discourse, the presentation of Cetshwayo as both intelligence supremo as well as generalissimo in battle was spread. The Zulu military machine was gaining the level of a cast conception in the public mind. The energetic Archibald Forbes was also making a living on the war, lecturing wherever and whenever he could, and he confirmed the view of the war that everyone at home wanted to hear: gallantry and heroism. He told an audience at the Drill Hall in Derby in February 1880 that one of the causes of the initial failure was the sheer weight of food carried with the army, and the reporter added, 'He believed that the British army should be well fed, but the best meal a soldier ever had was scraps of beef grilled on ramrods with a sprinkling of gunpowder for seasoning.'[154] But again, he was at pains to describe and pay tribute to the Zulu military prowess.

In the more popular journals, with family readers, there were tales of Shaka and accounts of the Zulu military habits and ideologies. But the most powerful and influential advocate and popularizer was Rider Haggard. His draft dedication of *Child of Storm*, for instance, has this passage:

> To serve their country in arms, to die for it, and for the king; such was their primitive ideal. If they were fierce, they were

> loyal, and feared neither wounds nor doom; if they listened to the dark redes of the witch doctors, the trumpet-call of duty sounded still louder in their ears ... From those who continually must face the last great issues of life and death, meanness and vulgarity are far removed.[155]

AGAINST SEKUKUNI

As a coda to the wars against the Zulus, Wolseley's campaign on Sekukuni, chief of the Bapedi, is also a fruitful case study in how Sir Garnet managed his intelligence arm. To the north-east of the Transvaal, bordering the Boer country, Sekukuni had created a massive stronghold for his warlike people. He had a central 'fighting kopje' in the heart of what many thought of as a land of thorns, sand and rocks. He had 4,000 armed men on that hill, and then radiating around this was a series of valleys and steep mountains. Inside the kopje were a number of caves where he could keep stores. The Bapedi liked to defend and to ambush rather than to be the aggressors.

In this situation, Wolseley, as the new governor who had supervised the mopping-up operations against the Zulu after Ulundi, was fully aware of the antagonism of the Boer settlers as well as the threat from Sekukuni. The Boers had pressed for independence time and again after the 1877 annexation, and had sent representatives to London. But now Sir Garnet decided to tour the place and speak, where he could, to make the situation clear. His biographer describes the situation: 'Sir Garnet boldly told them that annexation was irrevocable. As the Boers listened with in quiet and indignation, he assured them in his strong, stern voice that the sun would cease to shine and the Vaal would flow backwards before the British flag would be hauled down in this land.'[156] Wolseley knew that it was absolutely imperative to defeat Sekukuni for all kinds of reasons. It was basically a matter of pride, but also a victory would mean a renewal of faith in the imperial ideal and enterprise in the Transvaal.

He first played for time, sending a message to Sekukuni that offered a solution – a British presence close by his fort. This was rebuffed and there had to be a war with him. Wolseley had Henry Brackenbury with him now: a genius of military intelligence affairs who had taken the place of Colley on the general staff after the former was called to an emergency in Afghanistan. So confident was Wolseley with Brackenbury in his team that he boasted he would sip tea in Sekukuni's stronghold on 28 November. He was quite right: he did. The Transvaal Field Force was assembled for the campaign, but first Brackenbury got to work. The intelligence phase, preparatory to the assault on the Bapedi, involved liaison with the best sources of information about Sekukuni: the Reverend Merensky, a missionary and skilled cartographer, and Colonel Ignatius Ferreira, a Boer leader who was vastly experienced in warfare in Africa.

Brackenbury had received his first commission in the Royal Artillery in 1856, and had then been in the Central Indian Campaign of 1857–1858. The turning point for him – one that formed his career in intelligence – was his visit to the sites of the Franco-Prussian war in 1871 with the Society for the Aid of the Sick and Wounded. As private secretary to Wolseley in the Gold Coast in 1873 he had become a key member of the Ring. He was later, in 1883, to become military attaché in Paris. Therefore his experience in the field here in Africa, together with his interest in the theory of war derived from the Prussian experience, made him one of the few top men in military intelligence in the later Victorian army.

The plan, given full details of the topography of the Bapedi fortress, was a version of the Persian success at Thermopylae against the Spartans: it involved a reconnaissance of alternative routes into the kopje so that there would be the element of surprise. Native auxiliaries were also assembled; Wolseley and Brackenbury gathered forces from Swazis, Mapock's Kaffirs, Rustenburg levies and more. The Swazis were established enemies of the Bapedi, so that was a great advantage.

The column was ready after issues of transportation were settled and the decision made to attack by means of marching up the river Oliphant and descend from the Lulu mountains, so the fort would be stormed at the south. Supply obstacles were sorted out with a supply line put in place from Pretoria to the Oliphant, close to Fort Albert Edward. Lieutenant Colonel Baker Russell was to lead the column with Captain Herbert Stewart as staff officer – Russell being one of his former gang against the Ashanti. They were 500 miles from Durban, so supply plans and secondary actions had to be prepared with care. Wolseley and Ferreira's men conducted a reconnaissance; they decided that Major Bushman was to shell the kopje until he was to attack from the east later in the day. But there was an awful storm, and the correspondent from *The Telegraph*, Billy Russell, feared the worst. He could not have been more wrong. The concerted assault began, and Colonel Ferreira attacked from the right, while Major Carrington led the native contingents to clear the settlement. On top of that, the main assault was led by Colonel Murray and the 21st Royal Scots Fusiliers. Bushman and the Swazis then did a night attack to the east.

The attack began in the early hours of the morning and there was intense engagement, with some shifting of auxiliaries to give support where it was most urgently needed. But it did not take long to clear out and then burn the heart of the stronghold. There was a tough resistance at Sekukuni's kraal and it was in this scrap that Maurice was shot, as recalled in chapter 7. Wolseley was heard to say, 'Now I know the value of Maurice – to lead forlorn hopes!' The first phase – to attack the centre and hit it hard – took three hours and then Russell led a second wave from the plain. The Swazis took part in that, along with Murray's men, and after a rocket signal Russell gathered everyone and led the charge. Wolseley's biographer describes the decisive role of the Swazis at that point:

> The Swazis now ran as if death were behind them rather than before them. They answered the English cheer with their own battle-cry and made the same peculiar whish sound by striking their knees against their lowered shields as did the Zulus when they charged. Thousands of knees pounding in unison had the sound of roaring surf ...[157]

The kopje gave the attackers cover, in fact, and by half past ten in the morning, Sekukuni was beaten. All that remained in defiance was a knot of men with Sekukuni in the bowels of the hill. In another storm warriors ran out in a desperate rush to escape the British cordon.

Sekukuni was one who got through. Later, the chief was hounded into another cave and after a short siege he surrendered.

Wolseley had no rest. The Boers were ready to fight then. But at least it had been shown to the world that Britain had beaten the Zulu and Sekukuni, the bandit king of his nasty corner of the Transvaal. The campaign had been an object lesson in how all aspects of intelligence from field to fluid, and from information-gathering to liaison with and use of local knowledge, led to success. Marked contributions had been made by Brackenbury and Maurice. Wolseley, as always according to reports and memoirs, provided more than planning and confidence: he exuded geniality and good morale when needed and firmness with a touch of relentless self-belief in all important moments. Surely he had learned, along with most other military commentators, what the military correspondent of *The Times* wrote in 1880 about a fight with the Basutos: that the Zulus were unique. After all, his victory over Sekukuni had been totally unlike Chelmsford's campaign. The correspondent wrote of the Basutos: 'They are not soldiers like the Zulus were before the Zulus were broken up, but are merely hardy mountaineers.'[158]

12

Conclusions

The Anglo-Zulu War of 1879 may be assessed now from different standpoints when it comes to seeing where that conflict stands in relation to the development of military intelligence. From one position it is perhaps only a small piece in a very large jigsaw, but it may also be seen as something of a catalyst acting towards greater change. As has been seen, it was arguably one of the last stages of the prominence of wars fought almost entirely with humint intelligence. The technology was minor. Yet the individuals such as Brackenbury, Maurice, Dunn, Fynn, Clery and Buller (amongst many others) exemplified outstanding qualities of thought, planning and communications which are all central to field intelligence.

What happened after the conflict in terms of the wider sphere of intelligence has already been discussed. But a summary of developments is needed.

In 1887 the official Army Estimates, reported in the press, stated that the cost of administration at the War Office had increased by £2,600 that year. In that report there was an explanation of cost-cutting, including this note: 'The military clerks have been increased by 65. By these savings the expenditure on the Intelligence Branch and of the Works Branch has produced a net increase of only £6,800 in 22 years.'[159] This small detail suggests quite the wrong attitude. Eight years after the Anglo-Zulu War and other setbacks across the Empire, someone was trying to save pennies in the Intelligence Branch. But conversely and a little paradoxically, there was a burgeoning interest in military theory, and the War Office played its part in establishing the new attitudes.

The Times military correspondent in 1891 noted that a supposedly influential book written by a German officer, General Verdy du Vernois, who had been the War Minister of the German Empire, had been translated into English by a Captain J Grierson R A and published by the War Office. Grierson was in the Intelligence Branch. The book was then thought to be 'a new method of teaching the art of war.' In effect, Wolseley's formerly massive influence on the practical side of intelligence was being challenged by the academics. Only a few years before, with Wolseley's influence apparent, Captain R F Johnston of the Intelligence Branch lectured on 'Night Attacks in War' at the Royal United Services Institution. Officers in the colleges and in the offices in Whitehall were starting to analyze in new ways, reflecting soberly on past campaigns, earnest, committed and theoretical. That was a world away from the tough, enterprising art of war in the fields and hills of Zululand.

Following this line of thought, it becomes clear that the ongoing narrative of the confrontation with Cetshwayo was something that had not really been sidelines: on the contrary, those flights were filed under the relevant topics in the great filing cabinet of imperial struggles, there to be used, studied and hopefully used as military exemplars.

A summary of the nature of the field and theoretical intelligence of 1878–1879 has to include a solid tranche of criticisms, but most are futile as they are expressed with the wisdom of hindsight. Taking a broader view of Chelmsford's command and the whole enterprise, it becomes clear that at the very heart of the failures and shortcomings were three profound elements:

(a) South Africa was marginal in the Empire in the sense that other hotspots of war were prioritized.

(b) In turn, this meant that Frere and Bulwer, along with Hicks Beach in the first phase of ante-war debate, had time and power to create a platform for war.

(c) There was no streamlining and real communication in terms of the intelligence command. In fact it was not separately defined – nor was it in any theatre of war except in India.

(d) Because the range of skills and activities which would be rationalized and united later in the century were disjointed in 1879, there were poor levels of communication in most areas.
(e) In the context of diplomatic intelligence sources, there was nothing to equate Zululand or Natal with other locations in the Empire. It was unique in every way.

Taking all these factors into consideration, there is no doubt that Chelmsford turned things around in the five months after Isandlwana. But as the man chosen to replace him was Wolseley, there was never going to be a redemption of the scapegoat on the scene. Then, in the Sekukuni campaign, as Wolseley's methods proved to be successful, that was always going to overshadow the battles occurring between Isandlwana and Ulundi.

In the broad history and development of military intelligence in the last three decades of the nineteenth century, it is inevitable that the situation in southern Africa will be seen and appraised in its place within the geopolitics of the whole Empire and its trajectory, as intelligence work was raised more prominently into the areas of (a) integrated work done by military attachés and (b) specialized intellience officers with briefs of both information-gathering and wider cultural study of enemy states.

Uderlying all this, however, there is the undeniable hue of romance colouring the subject. In fact, the old male romance of the late Victorian novelists William Le Queux, Rider Haggard and Conan Doyle have all played their part in this. But at the centre of the arena here is the mix of the romance of 'spying' and the straightforward military duties we would term 'intelligence'. This means that the word 'espionage' in the context of the Victorian imperial quest covers several elements, all a part of the scene. The sources of military information available during this period include activities as diverse as map-making and surveying; amateur scholars supplying cultural information; linguists and travellers who learned about the enemy, though in a desultory manner; personnel within the army, for a long period the ranks of the engineers; political officers on missions; and most fundamental of all, native ranks and civilians such as the 'pundits' employed by the administration of the Raj.

All this summatory thinking relates to the point that field and fluid intelligence need immediate responses, either to be discarded (as Chelmsford often did, and so he noted in letters and logs) or to be trusted, with that trust based on past experience or familiarity with the provenance of the source. These hard lessons, tried and tested in the Crimea, had not been dragged out of context and assessed, ready for integration into the new Intelligence Branch in the late 1870s: that would have been asking too much of a section of the army still defined as inessential and of less importance than strategy and tactics, ordnance and munitions, drill and training. If we take a cursory look down the years before the war of 1879 then we see a succession of conflicts in which every commander had to rely on a range of sources of local information. This was notoriously fluid and so untrustworthy; generals had become accustomed to placing more reliance on the mixture of amateur information, given by such people as missionaries or magistrates, and the statements from scouting parties. But these did not include any in-depth profiles such as a military gazetteer would supply.

The result was that, without a foundation of accredited knowledge of enemy, terrain and cultural or ideological factors, a military decision would inevitably be risky, but within the known parameters established by previous actions, somewhat like a decision in a court of law, based on precedence. On top of that was trial and error and the occasional innovation, such as rocket batteries in the Napoleonic War or indeed the heliostat or heliograph as figured against the Zulus. However, Ulundi verified these established approaches, the square and the forays by cavalry proving to be decisively triumphant.

As time passed after the capture of Cetshwayo and the later problems with the Boers, it became apparent that issues of intelligence with regard to the British army took second place to the sheer timeless spying on home ground done by Zulu spies. The capture of the spy by Maurice during the hunt for the fugitive Cetshwayo proves the futility of that element of warfare: the man simply lied and led Maurice on a wild goose chase. What could be more naïve and misleading than the *Illustrated London News* pictures (from Melton Prior) showing cavalry searching for spies after the death of the Prince Imperial, or the picture of Newdigate interrogating a captured spy? These images relate to no proven success. Threats and physical punishment could be made all day long, yet captured spies could still invent fanciful tales and smile.

For all these reasons, the story of military intelligence in the Anglo-Zulu War is one of small successes and large failures, redeemed largely by determination, established British tactics and technology. It appears throuth the lens of time like the last of the imperial narratives in which a tribal state rattled and belittled a European army, and its dominant stories are those of individuals, rather than of complex strategy or any master plan. It comes as no surprisc that the developments in the administration of intelligence sources and records came partly from amateurs and partly from the new breed of officers in the decades after the war. The well-known split between the 'African Ring' following Wolseley and the 'Indian Ring' following Roberts highlights the comparison very clearly between the two locations of imperial conflict: by the 1830s the Indian locations across the sub-continent had the framework of the army of the East India Company as well as a network of magistrates across the native states; southern Africa merely had a motley assemblage of colonists.

The Wolseley Ring had, in one way, learned their trade as tacticians and theorists from a mix of field experience against various indigenous peoples, whereas at least there was some common ground in the armies of the various Indian states who caused problems for Britain. There was, of course, the huge difference between the two with regard to Russia and the perceived threats which were part of the Great Game. Natal and the Transvaal must have seemed to the distant diplomats and administrators to be something of a 'throwback' to former times, or at most a borderline bundle of mixed groups of native tribes, each presenting mere tribulations on the great red map of Empire. How wrong this mindset was in the context of the Zulu military structures and in the inheritors of Shaka's values and culture. That peculiar fusion of cosmopolitan issues and localized political conditions made the Zulu War a unique case study in the history of military intelligence.

Behind all the military developments through the Victorian period there were the diplomatic; for that we have to see what the Foreign

Office was like in the years after the Crimea and as the Great Game escalated. There were permanent under-secretaries, recently studied by Keith Neilson and T G Otte, who have written that 'The Permanent Under Secretaries were part of the British governing elite, recruited from a very narrow base,' and they have described how, after 1871, there were entrance examinations for potential Foreign Office employees. Before that, we have testimony in various memoirs about the Foreign Office and comments about Africa in that respect are negative. Lord Redesdale, for instance, who joined the Office in 1858, wrote in his memoirs:

> Even American affairs, until the war broke out between North and South, aroused little interest, and as for Africa, there was only one man who took any heed of it, and his voice was a cry in the wilderness. There was none to hear and poor Wylde's minutes were buried without hope of resurrection in the campo santo of the Record Office.[164]

Clearly, by 1871 there was need of a shake-up, and the Foreign Office had to move into the age of efficiency, but regarding the events of 1879, like the Intelligence Branch, it was moving slowly into something more in line with Prussian thinking, and in fact Redesdale recounts just as much interest (and genuine education about war) in the 1870 war as was found in the Staff College at the time. We can understand the importance of the Foreign Office with regard to the nature of wars at the time when we look at Redesdale's comments on the Franco-Prussian War:

> War was the birth of a moment. There had been no hidden warlike preparations either in France or in Germany; indeed so little was this the case that Bismarck tells us that it was not until he had consulted Moltke [the Prussian field marshal] as to the relative states of the French and Prussian armies ... that he lighted the torch.[165]

There is surely no better insight into the intricate network of diplomacy, theoretical intelligence and the advent of war than this – a perception from inside the workings of politics and warfare at a time when the German empire was beginning to look towards Africa.

In practical terms this means that military intelligence for this seventy years was diverse, piecemeal, chaotic and massively amateur. What was needed was some method of classification and systemic implementation of knowledge. What happened was, until the last few decades of the century, very much a pragmatic process; ad hoc information was gained in any way possible. Of course there are several reasons for this slow and haphazard scale of change, one being that the sheer vastness of the Empire, the pink on the map, was the main feature. In a world map included in a geography textbook published in 1908 the Empire's pink stands out, bold and prominent: the Dominion of Canada, British Guiana, nine Africa possessions, India, Australasia and another forty island or smaller places.

As George Aston said in his account of the growth of the Intelligence Department, the southern African experience caused the British public to take an interest in army reform. The Intelligence Department was strengthened and staff increased. Once again, what the fiasco of the maps and the armaments proved was that the long history of the army's pragmatic approach to both field and resource intelligence was just not acceptable. One obvious, if simplistic, explanation of the failures in the campaign is that there was an attitude of assuming that one good, disciplined British soldier was worth six amateurs. How wrong that proved to be, the records show very clearly.

Yet in the most fundamental nature of military intelligence – the fluid movement of unproven knowledge in the field – the Anglo-Zulu War represents a string of successes, the more remarkable because the officers and men involved were not the new breed of men who were fond of statistics and filing. Codification and data-collection belong to the later age, the time of mechanized warfare. It is no accident that the *Official Narrative of the Field Operations Connected with the Zulu War* is a document created by a very new Intelligence Branch, an outfit with a rather muddled sense of itself. William Robertson, destined to become Field Marshall Robertson, was a key figure in the rise of that branch, and his memoirs represent an ever-changing beast, ridden by different masters for decades, never sure of what race it was in and rarely clear as to its destination. Robertson was well equipped, though: he passed the exams in

Hindustani as well as strategy, and had been taken to tour the battlefields of the Franco-Prussian War. He was the coming man of his time, albeit self-made, rising through the ranks. Though he was prominent in the much-prized Eastern Empire, he, like most of his peers, needed more than a gentle nudge to spend time thinking about a little-known military nation in southern Africa, destined to shake the *Pax Britannica* as much as the most determined and warlike Pathans and Afghans.

Writing about military intelligence in the mid to late nineteenth century inevitably brings a sense of elusiveness, of disintegration; the various influential factors in the overall picture tend to slip away like mist in early sunlight. But hopefully there have been themes here, areas of interest integral to the range of elements composing the whole picture of military intelligence as it was conceived at that time. More than anything else, the subject resembles a Roman tessellated pavement: we may discern an image in focus but at times this blurs, as other, more marginal pieces change colour and take a more prominent place in the whole image.

At times the mapping and surveying takes centre stage; then scouting and reconnaissance emerge as something of major interest. At other times the more experimental or innovative intelligence enterprise will attract attention. Hence the time spent on ballooning and sun-signalling. But in the end, as Allan Mallinson has noted in his recent (2009) survey of the British army, imperial wars in the years from Clive to Wolseley were always an example of firepower against 'low-tech' opposition. Mallinson stresses this as being 'assymetrical warfare' – the low-tech versus the increasingly mechanized armies with evermore effective arsenals of deadly weapons and also mechanized back-up and supply (as in the war against Arabia in 1882 in the Sudan). Yet, in the Anglo-Zulu War we see the lancers at Ulundi wreaking as much destruction as the Gatling guns.[160]

It is also too facile to assess Sir Garnet Wolseley as the guru of all things concerned with intelligence. Although his famed Ring contained a focus on what might be termed information-centred strategic thinking, it was more than that suggests. John Laffin sums up Wolseley's basic thinking when he writes,

> Sir Garnet Wolseley took Cardwell's reforms about officers to logical conclusion in the field. Not the least of Wolseley's many achievements was the issue on 1 April, 1883 of the order, Squadron, Battery and Company Training. This revolutionary order marked the beginning of a systematic and efficient training ... Wolseley insisted that every officer, no matter what the size of his command, was wholly and personally responsible for its training.[161]

This was massively important for intelligence work in the 1880s, as it was the foundation of communications and the functioning as a tight unit so essential in the 'low-tech' enemy confrontations. If any specific unit had to think quickly and with a unified purpose, training precepts were the only remedy, and surely that had been proved more convincingly at Rorke's Drift than anywhere else in the 1879 war. Thinking centred on Royal Engineers' training was the foundation of that success, and that enabled the fighting to work with the necessary time and space, however tight that was between Zulu onslaughts.

This is not to say that field intelligence markedly improved by the last decade of the century: in the Anglo-Boer War it would be the same as ever. As Thomas Pakenham has it, with reference to 1899: 'The central problem ... to dominate the war was intelligence: where and how strong was the enemy? How strong was the invisible fence of steel, blocking the path between Kimberly and the Orange River?[162] In the preparations for the 1879 conflict, there was the massive central problem of the terrain, and also, something that is not often noted sufficiently, there was the issue of the nature of the native levies. The *Annual Register* for 1879 made a point of the importance of this with regard to the function of communications: 'The officers selected were of the various nationalities which the white communities of southern Africa offered. There were constant complaints that they were not familiar with Zulu usages, that they did not speak the Zulu language, and many of them could not speak English.'[163] This only refers to the general levies, not the special corps formed to work under regular officers.

The Anglo-Zulu War of 1879, when seen and understood as a small part of a massive rumbling machine called Empire, can be approached by means of purely battle-centred narrative, but it may also be looked at from other viewpoints, and hopefully this survey of all the factors affecting military intelligence will have opened up some new lines of thought. If a major consequence of the impact of intelligence at the highest level had to be discerned it might be to confirm Jeremy Black's words that 'For foreign states, the central narrative of the unprecedented projects of western power gave conflict the unintended effect of entwining hitherto separated societies more deeply ...'[66] Moreover, the consequences of the imperial wars in the 1870s were matters that brought about radical changes, and as Black observes, 'The potential gap between well- and poorly-structured and commanded militaries grew ...'[167] It was to be the Age of Wolseley until the Boers emerged to take on the might of Britain.

Previously, it has been a simple matter to place a war in context, but the political context of 1879 was so complex – being a mix of paranoia and myth – that the fear of Russia permeated most thinking in the embassies and in the service clubs. The pervading attitudes of a society's great narrative tend to work through to lower levels, and in this case that meant, ultimately, to Chelmsford and then to Wolseley. Understanding that perhaps explains some of the 'disasters' as well as of the bullying diplomacy of the southern African context in 1879.

Time Line

1855 The Topographical and Statistical Department established
1858–1863 Stieber reorganizes the Russian secret service
1860 The Committee on Military Organization, under Sir James Graham, created the following: the Commander in Chief made secondary to the Secretary of State; Horse Guards and the War Office to be together, under the same roof
1860 Russell of *The Times* publishes his Indian diary
1863 The death of Dost Mohammad
1864 Sir John Lawrence is appointed the Governor General of India
The Clerkenwell explosion kills thirteen people. Secret Service department created to protect London against Fenian bombings
1867 Army Reserve Act
1868 International Telegraph Convention
1869 Thomas Beach appointed assistant adjutant general of the Fenians
1870 Kitchener joins the Royal Engineers
1871 Unification of Germany – Bismarck in power
1872 The Cardwell reforms: regimental organization is restructured based on linked battalions, one serving at home and one abroad
1873–1874 Wolseley is victorious in the Ashanti War
1873 Khiva is occupied by Russian forces
1873 Intelligence Branch formed as part of the Quartermaster General's Department
1874 Opening of Suez Canal
1874–1880 Disraeli's second ministry

1875 Fred Burnaby makes his *Ride to Khiva*
1877 The Russo-Turkish War (23 January: resignation of Lord Carnarvon)
Annexation of the Transvaal (12 April)
1877–1879 Gordon Governor in the Sudan
1878 11 December: ultimatum given to Cetshwayo at Lower Thukela Drift
1878 Second Afghan War
1878 Treaty of the Congress of Berlin signed by Britain, along with all main European powers
1879 22 January: Isandlwana; 22 and 23 January: Rorke's Drift defence
1879 March 29: Zulu army attacks and is beaten at Khambula
1879 June 1: the Prince Imperial of France is killed
1879 July 4: Battle of Ulundi
1879 14 August: Wolseley takes chiefs' surrender; Cetshwayo taken on 28 August
1879 September: Third Afghan War
1880 Baden-Powell at Maiwand, becomes interested in tracking

Acknowledgements

Thanks are due to Dr Adrian Greaves, John Laband and Ian Knight, to whose work I owe a great deal here (as all writers on this war are bound to do). I also have to thank Adrian Greaves and Ian Knight for allowing me to use the nine illustrations, as credited in the illustrations section. The labours involved in this book were made much easier thanks to Ian Knight's invaluable *Companion to the Anglo-Zulu War*. This book has had, inevitably, to relate the events of one specific conflict to the big picture. Without the pioneering work of Richard Deacon and Christopher Andrew, this would have been difficult indeed. As a recent biography of William Melville has shown, details of individuals are elusive and piecemeal.

Particular thanks are due also to Lieutenant Colonel David Mullineaux for his writing on the heliograph in the *Journal of the Anglo-Zulu War Historical Society.*

Staff at King's College Library, The British Library, The East Riding Archives and the Lincolnshire Archives were extremely helpful. Also, the staff at the Special Collections of King's College were a great help in locating early printed sources. Talks with Guy Hallowes, descendant of Archdeacon Johnson of Uqutu, were also very beneficial, as were the many talks I had with South African friends on this subject.

Archivists Tim Stankus and Martin Skipworth at the Royal Signals Museum were very helpful in locating sources, and thanks to them I was able to consult a valuable monograph on the subject. At the National Army Museum, assistance regarding the Chelmsford papers from staff was invaluable.

Sources and Bibliography

Note: there is no doubt that there is now such a vast amount of information on the Anglo-Zulu War of 1879 that material on every conceivable aspect of the conflict grows daily. In terms of all the categories of intelligence I defined at the outset – localized, fluid, field and humint – most of the sources are fragmented and spread among the various first-hand and official accounts of the battles of the war. I have therefore confined my writing to that corpus of materials and sources which relates to any of the four categories above. I have not gone into great detail on the field intelligence, as that is recorded in abundance and is well understood.

Most of the bibliography will therefore relate to the theoretical, political and diplomatic dimensions of intelligence gathering as it was in the mid-Victorian years. Even the key contemporary text, the *Official History of the Field Operations*, though produced by the new Intelligence Branch, does not have a summatory analysis of scouting and reconnaissance, and that surely, more than any other factor, informs us of the lack of an intelligence staff with Chelmsford in any other capacity than an ad hoc one. There was nothing unusual in that within the army at the time. Although Wellington had used spies behind enemy lines in the Napoleonic War, that same operation would not have been possible in 1879 against the Zulu. Cetshwayo, of course, as recalled in chapter 9, certainly did have his spies within Natal.

The workings and thinking behind British military intelligence in the last thirty years of the nineteenth century had been largely ignored until T G Fergusson's book of 1984 (see below). My own *Spies in the Empire* was an attempt to add to that, and in researching that book I saw just how crucially important the Zulu War was for the way in which intelligence developed at all levels. For that reason I have included here works relating to foreign policy and diplomacy. The reason for this is that the military attaché became, as he had been in Russia since circa 1830, a part of the fabric of intelligence.

There tends to be a prominence given by publishers to strong dramatic narrative of course in the Victorian imperial wars; this has been to the detriment of the other many and varied aspects of army life. But that has been remedied somewhat by Ian Beckett, Allan Mallinson and Edward Spiers. Nevertheless, there remains the lacuna of military intelligence history in the decades between the end of the war with Napoleon and the Anglo-Boer War. John Keegan's *Intelligence in War*, dealing with that period, switches attention to Stonewall Jackson across the Atlantic. Until the autobiographies of men such as Sir William Robertson appeared, there was very little on that interim period in which the new branch was feeling its feet.

For these commercial reasons rather than historiographical ones, the writings on military intelligence in 1879 have been limited mainly to the journals, many of these being obscure. This is all understandable, as the dominance of Isandlwana in the writing on the war has meant that a common opinion has been sustained that there can have been no 'intelligence' if such a disaster happened. In particular, the *Journal of the Anglo-Zulu War Historical Society* is invaluable in this respect.

Going beyond the field intelligence narratives in order to find aspects of the various contextual factors in the diplomacy, from regional centres of power to the government agents, has meant reading between the lines, as there were so many biased opinions and vested interests. Because South Africa was hardly the priority in the early to mid 1870s in the minds of the diplomats and senior officers of the Indian Army or those at Cairo or Cyprus, there has been a certain amount of detective work, piecing together information by inference at times. I have had to follow Polonius's advice in Hamlet and 'By indirections find directions out,' so this entailed digging up long-forgotten memoirs, but it has to be said that this was really worthwhile.

Potentially, Sir Garnet Wolseley was a unique source, but as Donald R Morris wrote in *The Washing of the Spears* 'Sir Garnet Wolseley published a distressingly incomplete autobiography which stops in 1873 – just before he entered controversial waters' (p 621). A new, revisionary biography of the leader of the Ring is overdue.

SOURCES IN ARCHIVES

British Library Miscellaneous Public Documents CSD 1/5 24, February 1877,

On the Military Defences of South Africa: A Memorandum Addressed to the Government of the United Kingdom by Sir Bartle Frere (London, 1877)

British Parliamentary Papers, Natal 1878–1879 (HMSO)

Chelmsford Papers, National Army Museum

East Riding Archives, Saltmarshe Papers DDSA 1101

Fynney, F B, *Booklet on the Zulu Army.* National Army Museum 6610–45

Gladstone Papers in the British Library

Gloucester Record Office Hicks Beach Papers: Correspondence and Papers of Sir Michael Hicks Beach. Hicks Beach to Sir Garnet Wolseley D2455/PCC/7

King's College Library, LHCMH Archives, Sir John Frederick Maurice Papers

Lincolnshire Archives, Conyers Papers YARB 16/7/4 for the material on Sackville Lane-Fox

National Archives Ref 32/7717 to 32/7783

Parliamentary Papers for 1879, Transvaal

Royal Society, *W. de la Rue to Prof. Stokes* mss, letter Feb 1872, Memorandum on the Kew Heliograph: 'Relative to the Observations taken with the Kew heliograph', Department of Information: 10.1098 transcript 1871.0046

—— and Chree, C, Memorandum on the Kew Heliograph January 1916 10.1098/rspa 1916.0006

Salisbury Papers at Christ Church, Oxford

PRIMARY SOURCES: PRINTED

REPORTS AND BOOKS

Adye, Sir John, *Soldiers and Others I have Known* (London: Jenkins, 1925)

Aston, Sir George, *Secret Service* (London: Faber and Faber, 1930)

Baden-Powell, Robert, *Scouting for Boys*, ed Elleke Boehmer (Oxford: OUP, 2005)

——, 'My Adventures as a Spy' in *Fifty Amazing Secret Service Dramas* (London: Odhams, 1927), pp 180–206

British Almanac and Companion 1879 and 1880 (London: The Company of Stationers)

Brunskill, Ian (ed), *The Times Great Victorian Lives: An Era in Obituaries* (London: Times, 2007)

Bryant, A T, *Olden Times in Zululand and Natal* (Capetown: C Struik, 1965)

Burnaby, Frederick, *A Ride to Khiva*, ed and intro Peter Hopkirk (Oxford: OUP, 1997)

——, *On Horseback through Asia Minor* (London: Sampson Low, 1877)

Carnarvon Commission PRO CAB 7/2, First Report into the Defences of Commercial Harbours and Coaling Stations, 1877

Cunynghame, General Sir Arthur, *My Command in South Africa 1874–78* (London: Macmillan, 1879)

Dolby, I E A (ed), *Journal of the Household Brigade 1871* (London: Clowes, 1871)

Forbes, Archibald, *Barracks, Bivouacs and Battles* (London: Macmillan, 1894)

Greaves, Adrian and Best, Brian, *The Curling Letters of the Zulu War* (Barnsley: Pen and Sword, 2004)

Greaves, Sir George Richards, *Memoirs of General Sir George Greaves* (London: John Murray, 1924)

Haggard, H Rider, *Nada the Lily* (London: Longmans Green, 1933)

Hall, John and Burgis, Nina, *Anthony Trollope: The Letters* (Stanford: Stanford University Press, 1983)

Harrison, Sir Richard, *Recollections of a Life in the British Army* (London: Smith, Elder, 1908)

Hughes, William, *The Advanced Modern Geography* (London: George Philip, 1908)

Intelligence Branch of the Quartermaster-General's Department, War Offices 1880

Journal of the Household Brigade 1871 (London: W Clowes and Sons, reprinted Uckfield: The Naval and Military Press Ltd, 2000)

Maurice, Sir J F, *The Life of Lord Wolseley* (New York: Doubleday, 1924)

McCabe Lt Col M T 9RE and Burtenshaw, Mrs Cynthia, *The Recollections of Colonel R T Main*, transcribed in 1894

Narrative of the Field Operations connected with The Zulu War of 1879 (official history, reprinted Uckfield: The Naval and Military Press, 2000)

Norris-Newman, Charles, *In Zululand: With the British throughout the War of 1879* (London, 1880)

Parr, Captain H H, *Guadana to Isandlwana: A Sketch of the Zulu and Kaffir Wars* (London: Routledge and Kegan Paul, 1880)

Prior, Melton, *Campaigns of a War Correspondent* (London: Arnold, 1930)

Redesdale, Lord, *Memories* (New York: E P Dutton, 1915)

Robertson, Sir William, *From Private to Field Marshall* (London: Constable, 1921)

Russell, William Howard, *My Diary in India* (London: Routledge, Warne, 1860)

Steevens, G W, *With Kitchener to Khartoum* (Edinburgh: Blackwood, 1898)

Wilkinson, Spenser, *Thirty-Five Years 1874–1909* (London: Constable, 1933)

Wolseley, Field Marshall Viscount, *The Story of a Soldier's Life* (London: Constable, 1903, 2 vols)

ARTICLES IN JOURNALS AND PERIODICALS

Dolby, I E A, 'The Kriegspiel or Game of War', *The Journal of the Household Brigade*, 1871, pp 178–179

Forbes, Archibald, 'Lord Chelmsford and the Zulu War', *The Nineteenth Century*, February 1880, pp 90–96

——, 'War Correspondents and the Authorities', *The Nineteenth Century*, January 1880, pp 185–193
——, 'Wolseley: A Character Profile', *The English Illustrated Magazine*, 1884–1885, pp 516–521
Frere, Sir Bartle, 'The Turkish Empire', *Quarterly Review* 142, October 1876
Froude, J A, 'English Policy in South Africa', *Quarterly Review* 143, January 1877, p 107
Henderson, G B, 'Lord Palmerston and the Secret Service Fund', *English Historical Review* 53, 1938
Home Friend, Part VII, 1855 (London: Clowes and Son)
Wilkinson, Spenser, 'On Going to War', *Anglo-Saxon Review*, 1899

SECONDARY SOURCES

BOOKS

Allen, Charles, *Soldier Sahibs* (London: John Murray, 2000)
Beckett, Ian, *The Victorians at War* (London: Hambleton Continuum, 2006)
Biddle, George Earle, *The Life of Benjamin Disraeli, Earl of Beaconsfield* (London: John Murray, 1920)
Black, Jeremy, *Maps and History: Constructing Images of the Past* (Connecticut: Yale, 1997)
——, *Rethinking Military History* (London: Routledge, 2004)
Blake, Robert, *Disraeli* (London: Eyre and Spottiswoode, 1966)
Bodelsen, C A, *Studies in Mid-Victorian Imperialism* (London: Hutchinson, 1960)
Bonham-Carter, Victor, *Soldier True: The Life and Times of Sir William Robertson* (London: Frederick Muller, 1963)
Bott, Alan, *Our Fathers* (Heinemann, 1931)
Briggs, Asa, *Victorian People* (London: Penguin, 1973)
Bruce, Richard, *The Forward Policy and its Results* (London: Longman, 1900)
Chandler, David G and Beckett, Ian, *The Oxford History of the British Army* (Oxford: OUP, 1994)

Clayton, Anthony, *The British Officer: Leading the Army from 1660 to the Present Day* (Edinburgh: Pearson Longman, 2007)
Cope, Richard, *Ploughshare of War* (Pietermaritzburg: University of KwaZulu Natal Press, 1999)
Creswicke, Louis, *South Africa and the Transvaal War* (Edinburgh: T C Jack, 1900)
Crowdy, Terry, *The Enemy Within: A History of Espionage* (Oxford: Osprey, 2006)
Dasent, Arthur Irwin, *John Thaddeus Delane, Father of The Times: His Life and Correspondence* (New York: Scribner, 1908, vol 1)
David, Saul, *Military Blunders* (London: Robinson, 1995)
——, *Zulu* (London: Robinson, 1997)
Deacon, Richard, *The British Secret Service* (London: Grafton, 1991)
——, *A History of the Russian Secret Service* (London: Grafton, 1987)
Downer, Martyn, *The Queen's Knight* (London: Transworld, 2007)
Dowswell, Paul and Fleming, Fergus, *True Spy Stories* (London: Usborne, 2000)
Dunn, W H, *James Anthony Froude: A Biography* (Oxford: OUP, 1963)
Eliot, T S (ed), *A Choice of Kipling's Verse* (London: Faber, 1983)
Ferguson, Niall, *Empire* (London: Penguin, 2005)
Fergusson, T G, *British Military Intelligence 1870–1914* (New York: University Publications of America, 1984)
Farquhar, Michael, *A Treasury of Deception* (London: Penguin, 2005)
Ferris, John Robert, *Intelligence and Strategy: Selected Essays* (London: Routledge, 2005)
Field, Cyril, *Old Times Under Arms* (London: Hodge, 1929)
Fishlock, Trevor, *Conquerors of Time: Exploration and Invention in the Age of Daring* (London: John Murray, 2004)
Flexner, Doris and Berg, Stuart, *The Pessimist's Guide to History* (New York: Harper Collins, 2008)
Foot, M R D, *Secret Lives: Lifting the Lid on Worlds of Secret Intelligence* (Oxford: OUP, 2002)
Forbes, Archibald, Henry, G A and Griffiths, Major Arthur, *Battles of the Nineteenth Century* (London: Cassell, 1900, 6 vols)

French, Gerald, *Lord Chelmsford and the Zulu War* (London: John Lane, 1939)

Gilmour, David, *The Ruling Caste* (London: John Murray, 2005)

Gonzalez, Carlos Roca, *Isandlwana: The Bitter Zulu Victory* (South Africa: A F Editions, 2006)

Goodfellow, Clement Francis, *Great Britain and South African Confederation 1870–1881* (Cape Town: Oxford University Press, 1966)

Greaves, Adrian, *Rorke's Drift* (London: Cassell, 2002)

—— and Knight, Ian, *Who's Who in the Zulu War* (Barnsley: Pen and Sword, 2006, 2 vols)

Hackwood, F W, *The Life of Lord Kitchener* (London and Glasgow: Collins, 1918)

Haggard, H Rider, *Diary of an African Journey 1914* (London: Hurst, 2002)

——, 'A Farmer's Year', *Longman's Magazine* 1898–9 (later London: Cresset Press, 1967)

Hall, Sheldon, *Zulu: With Some Guts Behind It: The Making of an Epic Movie* (Sheffield: Tomahawk Press, 2005)

Hamilton, George, *Parliamentary Reminiscences and Reflections 1886–1906* (London: John Murray, 1922)

Harfield, Major A G, *The Heliograph* (Royal Signals Museum and Archives, Blandford Camp, 1981)

Haswell, Jock, *The British Army: A Concise History* (London: Thames and Hudson, 1975)

Hibbert, Christopher, *Queen Victoria: A Personal History* (London: Murray, 2000)

History of the Corps of Signals (Mhow, India: Corps of Signals Committee, 1975, vol 1)

Herman, Michael, *Intelligence Power in Peace and War* (Cambridge: CUP and Royal Institute of International Affairs, 2000)

Holmes, Richard (ed), *The Oxford Companion to Military History* (Oxford: OUP, 2001)

Hopkirk, Peter, *The Great Game* (Oxford: OUP, 1977)

Howse, Christopher (ed), *How We Saw It 1855–2005* (London, Ebury Press, 2005)

Hughes-Wilson, John, *The Puppet Masters* (London: Cassell, 2004)
Huizinga, Johan, *Homo Ludens* (London: Beacon Press, 1971)
Jeal, Tim, *Baden-Powell* (London: Hutchinson, 1999)
Johnson, R Brimley, *Popular British Ballads* (London: Dent, 1910)
Johnson, Robert, *Spying for Empire* (London: Greenhill, 2006)
Judd, Denis, *Someone has Blundered* (London: Orion, 1973)
Keay, John, *The Great Arc* (London: HarperCollins, 2000)
Kebbel, T E, *Lord Beaconsfield* (London: Constable, 1888)
Keegan, John, *Intelligence in War* (London: Pimlico, 2003)
Kipling, Rudyard, *Selected Poems* (London: Faber, 1983)
Knight, Ian, *Brave Men's Blood: The Epic of the Zulu War 1879* (Barnsley: Pen and Sword, 2005)
——, *Companion to the Anglo-Zulu War* (Barnsley: Pen and Sword, 2008)
——, *Rorke's Drift 1879* (Oxford: Osprey, 1996)
——, *The National Army Museum Book of the Zulu War* (London: Pan, 2004)
Knightley, P, *The First Casualty: The War Correspondent as Hero, Propagandist and Myth-Maker from the Crimea to Vietnam* (London: Andre Deutsch, 1975)
Laband, John, *Lord Chelmsford's Zululand Campaign 1878–1879* (Stroud: Sutton, 1994, for the Army Records Society)
——, *The Rise and Fall of the Zulu Nation* (London: Arms and Armour Press, 1997)
——and Knight, Ian, *The War Correspondents: The Anglo-Zulu War* (Stroud: Sutton, 1996)
Laffin, John, *Tommy Atkins: The Story of the English Soldier* (Stroud: Sutton, 2004)
Lehmann, Joseph, *All Sir Garnet: A Life of Field-Marshal Lord Wolseley* (London: Cape, 1964)
Longford, Elizabeth, *Victoria R I* (London: Weidenfeld and Nicolson, 1964)
Mallinson, Allan, *The Making of the British Army* (London: Bantam, 2009)
Martineau, John, *The Life and Correspondence of Sir Bartle Frere* (London: Constable, 1895)

Morris, Donald R, *The Washing of the Spears: The Rise and Fall of the Zulu Nation* (London: Jonathan Cape, 1965)
Morris, Jan, *Heaven's Command: An Imperial Progress* (London: Faber, 1998)
Nalson, David, *The Victorian Soldier* (Princes Risborough: Shire, 2004)
Nasson, Bill, *Britannia's Empire* (Stroud: Tempus, 2004)
Naylor, Major General R F H, *The Royal Corps of Signals* (London: Royal Signals Institution, 1958)
Neilson, Keith and Otte, T G, *The Permanent Under-Secretary for Foreign Affairs 1854–1946* (London: Routledge, 2009)
O'Connor, Damian P, *The Zulu and the Raj: a life of Sir Bartle Frere* (London: Able, 2002)
Pakenham, Thomas, *The Boer War* (London: Abacus, 1997)
Pollock, John, *Kitchener: The Road to Omdurman* (London: Constable, 1998)
Porter, A N, *Atlas of British Overseas Expansion* (London: Routledge, 1991)
Porter, Roy, *The Enlightenment* (London: Penguin, 2004)
Preston, Adrian (ed), *In Relief of Gordon: Lord Wolseley's Campaign Journal of the Khartoum Relief Expedition 1884–5* (London: Hutchinson, 1967)
Ramm, A, *Sir Robert Morier: Envoy and Ambassador in the Age of Imperialism* (Oxford: OUP, 1973)
Rayner, Ed and Stapley, Ron, *Debunking History* (Stroud: Sutton, 2002)
Rider Haggard, Lilias, *The Cloak that I Left: A Biography of H Rider Haggard* (London: Boydell Press, 1951)
Roberts, Andrew, *Salisbury: Victorian Titan* (London: Orion, 2000)
Robinson, Ronald and Gallagher, John, *Africa and the Victorians* (London: Macmillan, 1961)
Royle, Trevor, *Crimea* (London: Abacus, 1999)
Sarkissian, A O (ed), *Studies in Diplomatic History and Historiography in Honour of G P Gooch* (London: Macmillan, 1961)
Seth, Ronald, *The Encyclopaedia of Espionage* (New York: New English Library, 1972)

Signalling Training vol III pamphlet no 2: Heliograph (London: HMSO)

Spiers, Edward M, *The Late Victorian Army 1868–1902* (Manchester: Manchester University Press, 2002)

Steiner, Zara S, *The Foreign Office and Foreign Policy* (New York: CUP, 1969)

Sumner, *B H, Russia and the Balkans 1870–1880* (London: Constable, 1937)

Susan, Countess of Malmesbury, *The Life of Major-General Sir John Ardagh* (London: John Murray, 1909)

Sweet, Matthew, *Inventing the Victorians* (London: Faber and Faber, 2001)

Talbot-Booth, E C, *The British Army: Its History, Customs, Traditions and Uniforms* (London: Sampson Low, Marston, 1937)

Taylor, A J P, *The Struggle for Mastery in Europe 1848–1918* (London: Penguin 1954)

Taylor, Stephen, *Shaka's Children* (London: HarperCollins, 1987)

Teed, Peter and Clarke, Michael, *Portraits and Documents: Later Nineteenth Century 1868–1919* (London: Hutchinson, 1999)

Twigge, Stephen, Hampshire, Edward and Macklin, Graham, *British Intelligence: Secrets, Spies and Sources* (Kew: The National Archives, 2008)

Wade, Stephen, *Spies in the Empire* (London: Anthem, 2007)

Waldron, Peter, *The End of Imperial Russia, 1855–1917* (Basingstoke: Palgrave Macmillan, 1997)

Wilkinson, H Spenser, *Thirty-Five Years 1874–1909* (London: Constable, 1933)

Woods, David L, *A History of Tactical Communications Techniques* (Florida: Martin Company, Martin-Marietta Corporation, 1965)

Articles in Journals and on Websites

Annual Register September 1879, South Africa in Foreign News section

Atmore, A and Marks, S, 'The Imperial Factor in South Africa in the Nineteenth Century' in E F Penrose (ed), *New Orientations Series No 2: European Imperialism and the Partition of Africa* (London: Frank Cass, 1975)

Coan, Stephen, 'H Rider Haggard in Pagada's Kop', www.violetbooks.com, p 2

Dwyer, F J, 'R A Cross and the Eastern Crisis of 1875-8', off-print from the *Slavonic and East European Review*, vol XXXIX 93, June 1961

Hoskins, H L, 'British Policy in Africa 1873–1877: A Study in Geographical Politics', *Geographical Review* XXXII, 1942, pp 140–149

Knight, Ian, 'Ghosts of the Zulu War', *Military Illustrated* 249, February 2009, pp 32–39

Mullineaux, Lt Col David, 'Signalling in the Anglo-Zulu War 1879', *Journal of the Anglo-Zulu War Historical Society*, December 2004

O'Connor, Damian P, 'Imperial Strategy and the Anglo-Zulu War of 1879', *The Historian*, 22 June 2006, pp 284–303

Peers, Donald M, 'Colonial Knowledge and the Military of India', *Journal of Imperial and Commonwealth History* 33, 2, May 2005, pp 157–180

Penner, C D, 'Germany and the Transvaal before 1896', *Journal of Modern History*, 1940, pp 31–58

Powell, Lieutenant Colonel S H, 'The Formation of Signals Companies in India', *Army Review*, 1911, compiled for the RE General Staff

Schimmelpenninck, David H, 'Russian Military Intelligence on the Manchurian Front 1904–05', *Intelligence and National Security* vol 11, 1, January 1996, pp 22–31

Smith, Keith L, 'Major Graves and the Native Natal Contingent', *Journal of the Society for Army Historical Research*, vol 86, 348, Winter 2008, pp 297–308

Smith, Paul, 'From Splendour to Peril', *Times Literary Supplement*, 3 October 2009, p 27

'With the Irregulars in the Zulu War', *The Royal United Services Magazine*, vol XXIV, 380, March 1880

WEBSITES

www.africa-ata.org/zulu.htm
www.aim25.ac.uk/cats
www.azwrs.com

www.anglozuluwar.com
http://bartleby.com/reference/
http://www.british-history.ac.uk
http://www.dself.dsl.pipex.com/MUSEUM/COMMS/heliograph/heliograph.htm www.remuseum.org.uk
www.national-army-museum.ac.uk
www.royalengineers.com
www.rrw.org.uk
www.soldiersofthequeen.com (for more information about Edric Gifford VC including photos and extensive biographical material)
www.victorianweb.org/history/frere
www.victorianwarsforum
http://www.victorianamagazine.com

JOURNALS

Anglo-Saxon Review
Annual Register
Army and Navy Gazette
BBC History
Blackwood's Edinburgh Magazine
Contemporary Review
Fortnightly Review
Journal of the Anglo-Zulu War Historical Society
Journal of Imperial and Commonwealth History
Journal of the Society for Army Historical Research
Literary Review
Macmillan's Magazine
Pall Mall Gazette
Past and Present
Punch
Royal United Services Magazine
Strand
The Idler
Times Literary Supplement

DIGITAL SOURCES/NEWSPAPERS AND PERIODICALS

British History Online
British Nineteenth Century Newspapers
The Graphic
Illustrated London News
Penny Illustrated Paper
The Times Digital Archive
Westminster Review

Notes

1 Lincolnshire Archives, Conyers Papers YARB 16/7/4.
2 Ibid.
3 Ibid.
4 Ibid.
5 Ibid.
6 Ibid.
7 Ibid.
8 Ibid.
9 Ibid.
10 Ibid.
11 Ibid.
12 Ibid.
13 East Riding Archives, Saltmarshe Papers DDSA 1101.
14 Ibid.
15 Ibid.
16 Lilias Rider Haggard, *The Cloak that I Left: A Biography of H Rider Haggard* (London: Boydell Press, 1951), p 38.
17 Roy Porter, *The Enlightenment* (London: Penguin, 2004), p 151.
18 Niall Ferguson, *Empire* (London: Penguin, 2005), p 127.
19 Douglas M Peers, 'Colonial Knowledge and the Military of India', *Journal of Imperial and Commonwealth History* vol 33, 2, May 2005, p 157.
20 Ibid, p 174.
21 Ibid, p 163.
22 See Peter Waldron, *The End of Imperial Russia* (Basingstoke: Palgrave Macmillan, 1997), pp 139–147.
23 Rider Haggard, *The Cloak that I Left*, p 36.
24 Parliamentary Papers for 1879, Transvaal, p 308.
25 Ibid.

26 Ibid, p 309.
27 Ibid.
28 Ibid, p 310.
29 Ibid, p 312.
30 John Laband, *Lord Chelmsford's Zululand Campaign 1878–1879* (Stroud: Sutton, 1994, for the Army Records Society), p xviii.
31 Ibid, p 45.
32 *Narrative of the Field Operations Connected with The Zulu War of 1879* (official history, reprinted by the Naval and Military Press, Uckfield 2000), p 36.
33 Ibid, p 33.
34 Ibid, p 36.
35 Adrian Greaves and Brian Best, *The Curling Letters of the Zulu War* (Barnsley: Pen and Sword, 2004), p 94.
36 Chelmsford Papers, National Army Museum, p 87.
37 Ibid, p 71.
38 See George Earle Biddle, *The Life of Benjamin Disraeli, Earl of Beaconsfield* (London: John Murray, 1920), p 424.
39 Forbes in Archibald Forbes, G A Henry and Major Arthur Griffiths, *Battles of the Nineteenth Century* (London: Cassell, 1900), vol 2, p 263.
40 Ibid, p 219.
41 Ibid, p 221.
42 *The Times*, letters, 3 February 1879.
43 *The Times*, 19 February 1879, letter from Lovell Proctor.
44 *The Times*, 18 February 1879, letter from 'Elcho'.
45 Ibid, from Robert Gunther.
46 Ibid, from Walter Woodbury.
47 Forbes, Henry and Griffiths, *Battles of the Nineteenth Century*, p 624 (article by C Stein).
48 *Narrative of the Field Operations*, p 53.
49 See ibid, p 56.
50 Chelmsford Papers, p 217.
51 See Ian Knight, *The National Army Museum Book of the Zulu War* (London: Pan, 2004), p 58.

52 *Narrative of the Field Operations*, p 77.
53 Ibid, p 116.
54 King's College Library, LHCMH archives, Sir John Frederick Maurice papers.
55 Chelmsford Papers, p 225.
56 Ibid, p 226.
57 See Biddle, *The Life of Benjamin Disraeli*, p 420.
58 Maurice Papers.
59 Ibid.
60 Ibid.
61 Ibid.
62 See Ian Knight, *Companion to the Anglo-Zulu War* (Barnsley: Pen and Sword, 2008), entry on Cetshwayo for a succinct account of this.
63 Sir J F Maurice, *The Life of Lord Wolseley* (New York: Doubleday, 1924), p 120.
64 John Hughes-Wilson, *The Puppet Masters* (London: Cassell, 2004), p 212.
65 Sir William Robertson, *From Private to Field Marshall* (London: Constable, 1921), p 91.
66 George Aston, *Secret Service* (London: Faber and Faber, 1930), p 20.
67 Joseph Lehmann, *All Sir Garnet: A Life of Field-Marshal Lord Wolseley* (London: Cape, 1964), p 233.
68 Ibid, p 244.
69 Robertson, *From Private to Field Marshall*, p 83.
70 Lehmann, *All Sir Garnet*, p 301.
71 Ibid, p 307.
72 Ibid, pp 167–168.
73 Maurice Papers.
74 See Knight, *Companion to the Anglo-Zulu War*, entry on Dunn.
75 Donald R Morris, *The Washing of the Spears: The Wise and Fall of the Zulu Nation* (London: Jonathan Cape, 1965), p 339.
76 Chelmsford Papers, p 83.
77 Tim Jeal, *Baden-Powell* (London: Hutchinson, 1999), p 133.

78 Adrian Greaves and Ian Knight, *Who's Who in the Zulu War* (Barnsley: Pen and Sword, 2006), vol 2, pp 33–42.
79 General Sir Arthur Cunynghame, *My Command in South Africa 1874–75* (London, Macmillan, 1879), p 34.
80 See www.africa-ata.org/zulu.htm.
81 William Howard Russell, *My Diary in India* (London: Routledge, Warne, 1860), p vii.
82 Matthew Sweet, *Inventing the Victorians* (London: Faber and Faber, 2001), pp 68–69.
83 Archibald Forbes, 'War Correspondents and the Authorities', *The Nineteenth Century*, January 1880, p 193.
84 Ibid, p 188.
85 Ibid.
86 Ibid, p 189.
87 Robert Blake, *Disraeli* (London: Eyre and Spottiswoode, 1966), p 671.
88 Martyn Downer, *The Queen's Knight* (London: Transworld, 2007), p 414.
89 Colonel William Fielding, letter to *The Times*, 12 March 1879.
90 Chelmsford Papers, p 221.
91 Charles Norris-Newman, *In Zululand: With the British throughout the War of 1879* (London, 1880), p 1.
92 Ibid, p v.
93 See, for example, the series of books by Cassell – Forbes, Henry and Griffiths, *Battles of the Nineteenth Century*, 6 vols.
94 *Natal Mercury*, 25 January 1879.
95 Rudyard Kipling, 'Fuzzy-Wuzzy', in *Selected Poems* (London: Faber, 1983), p 145.
96 Cunynghame, *My Command in South Africa*, p 344.
97 Robert Baden-Powell, *Scouting for Boys*, ed Elleke Boehmer (Oxford: OUP, 2005), p 152.
98 Forbes, 'War Correspondents and the Authorities', p 192.
99 See John Laband, *Lord Chelmsford's Zululand Campaign 1878–1879* (Stroud: Sutton, 1994, for the Army Records Society), p 220.
100 John Hall and Nina Burgis, *Anthony Trollope: The Letters* (Stanford: Stanford University Press, 1983), p 826.

101 Damian P O'Connor, 'Imperial Strategy and the Anglo-Zulu War of 1879', *The Historian* 68, 22 June 2006, pp 285–304.
102 Frederick Burnaby, *A Ride to Khiva*, ed and intro Peter Hopkirk (Oxford: OUP, 1997), p 70.
103 Frederick Burnaby, *On Horseback through Asia Minor* (London, Sampson Low, 1877), p 76.
104 Ibid, p 186.
105 Richard Deacon, *A History of the Russian Secret Service* (London: Grafton, 1987), p 102.
106 See David H Schimmelpenninck, 'Russian Military Intelligence on the Manchurian Front 1904–05', *Intelligence and National Security* 11, 1, January 1996, p 24.
107 O'Connor, 'Imperial Strategy', p 289.
108 Ibid, p 292.
109 This is quoted in Richard Cope, *Ploughshare of War* (Pietermaritzburg: University of KwaZulu Natal Press, 1999), p 239.
110 Frere to the Queen, 10 February 1879.
111 See O'Connor, 'Imperial Strategy', p 300.
112 See The Berlin Conference: General Act of 26 February 1885 on http: web.jjay.cuny.edu/jobrien.
113 O'Connor, 'Imperial Strategy', p 304.
114 *Blackwood's Edinburgh Magazine*, October 1878, p 490. This is but one note in a long feature on Russia's continued expansion, with references to supposed agreements broken etc.
115 See Tim Jeal, *Baden-Powell* (London: Hutchinson, 1999), p 174.
116 Robert Baden-Powell, 'My Adventures as a Spy' in *Fifty Amazing Secret Service Dramas* (London: Odhams, 1927), p 183.
117 Ibid, p 185.
118 *Narrative of Field Operations*, pp 91–92.
119 Trevor Fishlock, *Conquerors of Time: Exploration and Invention in the Age of Daring* (London: John Murray, 2004), p 240.
120 Major General R F H Naylor, *The Royal Corps of Signals* (London: Royal Signals Institution, 1958), p 20.

121 Royal Society, *W de la Rue to Prof. Stokes* mss, letter Feb 1872, Memorandum on the Kew heliograph: 'Relative to the Observations taken with the Kew heliograph' Doi: 10.1098 transcript 1871.0046.
122 Naylor, *The Royal Corps of Signals*, p 2.
123 Lieutenant Colonel David Mullineaux, 'Signalling in the Anglo-Zulu War 1879', *Journal of the Anglo-Zulu War Historical Society* (December 2004), p 24.
124 Ibid, p 14.
125 Ibid, p 15.
126 Ibid, p 16.
127 Quoted ibid, pp 16–17.
128 Quoted ibid, p 18, from *The Journal of the United Services Institution* vol XXIV, p 256.
129 McCabe Lt Col M T 9RE and Burtenshaw, Mrs Cynthia, *The Recollections of Colonel R T Main*, transcribed in 1894 (document in the library of the Royal Engineers).
130 H Baden Pritchard, *British Almanac and Companion* 1880 (London: The Company of Stationers).
131 *Illustrated London News* 1879, p 426.
132 Ibid, p 426.
133 G Dodd, *British Almanac and Companion* 1879 (London: The Company of Stationers).
134 See online exhibition of The Royal Engineers at www.remuseum.org.uk/.
135 *The Daily Graphic*, 5 June 1890, p 12.
136 Spenser Wilkinson, 'On Going to War', *Anglo-Saxon Review*, 1899.
137 Spenser H Wilkinson, *Thirty-Five Years 1874–1909* (London: Constable, 1933), p 113.
138 John Crowdy, 'South Africa', in *British Almanac and Companion* 1880, p 77.
139 Alan Bott, *Our Fathers* (Heinemann, 1931), p 116.
140 Archibald Forbes, 'Wolseley: A Character Sketch', *Anglo-Saxon Review* 1899, p 519.

141 Forbes, Henry and Griffiths, *Battles of the Nineteenth Century*, see C Stein, p 219.
142 See Crowdy, 'South Africa', p 77.
143 William Robertson, *From Private to Field Marshall* (London: Constable, 1921), p 100.
144 Ibid, p 130.
145 Anthony Clayton, *The British Officer: Leading the Army from 1660 to the Present Day* (Edinburgh: Pearson Longman, 2007), p 103.
146 John Pollock, *Kitchener: The Road to Omdurman* (London: Constable, 1998), p 41.
147 *The Times*, 26 October 1885, 'The Afghan Frontier Commission'.
148 Review in *Westminster Review*, April 1879, 'Our South African Colonies', p 187.
149 See Crowdy, 'South Africa', p 73.
150 R Brimley Johnson, *Popular British Ballads.*
151 Edward Durnford to *The Times*, 27 August 1880.
152 Reported and quoted in *The Literary Examiner*, 4 September 1880.
153 H Rider Haggard, *Nada the Lily* (London: Longmans Green, 1933), Introduction, p xi.
154 'Mr Archibald Forbes on the Zulu War', *Derby Mercury*, 11 February 1880.
155 Rider Haggard, *The Cloak that I Left*, p 54.
156 Lehmann, *All Sir Garnet*, p 262.
157 Ibid, p 273.
158 *The Times*, 1 September 1880, from the war correspondent.
159 See *The Times*, October 1887.
160 See Allan Mallinson, *The Making of the British Army* (London: Bantam, 2009), pp 238–239.
161 John Laffin, *Tommy Atkins: The Story of the English Soldier* (Stroud: Sutton, 2004), p 179.
162 Thomas Pakenham, *The Boer War* (London: Abacus, 1997), p 178.

163 'South Africa: Preliminaries to the War', *Annual Register* 1879, p 225.
164 Lord Redesdale, *Memories* (New York: E P Dutton, 1900), p 112.
165 Ibid, p 110.
166 Jeremy Black, *Rethinking Military History* (London: Routledge, 2004), p 181.
167 Ibid.

Index